The Invisible Spectrum

A Woman's Journey to Late Autism Diagnosis and Self-Discovery

Gaetana Yo Tate

This book is intended for informational and educational purposes only. The content provided is not intended to be a substitute for professional medical advice, diagnosis, or treatment. Always seek the advice of your physician or other qualified health provider with any questions you may have regarding a medical condition, including autism spectrum disorder.

The information in this book is based on research, clinical experience, and personal accounts, but individual experiences may vary significantly. Never disregard professional medical advice or delay in seeking it because of something you have read in this book.

If you think you may have autism spectrum disorder or any other medical condition, please consult with a qualified healthcare professional for proper evaluation and diagnosis.

To protect privacy and confidentiality, all personal names, case studies, and identifying details of individuals mentioned in this book have been changed or are composite representations based on multiple experiences. Any resemblance to actual persons, living or deceased, or actual events is purely coincidental.

The case studies and examples presented are created for illustrative purposes and represent common experiences reported by individuals with autism spectrum disorder. They should not be considered as typical or guaranteed outcomes.

Professional names, research citations, and clinical references mentioned throughout this book are used for educational and informational purposes only. Inclusion of any professional's work or research does not constitute endorsement of this book or its content by those individuals or their affiliated institutions.

Information regarding legal rights, workplace accommodations, and disability law is provided for educational purposes only and should not be considered legal advice. Laws vary by jurisdiction and change over time. Readers should consult with qualified legal professionals for specific legal guidance regarding their individual circumstances.

The accommodation strategies and templates provided are suggestions based on common successful approaches but may not be appropriate for all situations or jurisdictions.

The publisher and author make no representations or warranties with respect to the accuracy or completeness of the contents of this book and specifically disclaim any implied warranties of merchantability or fitness for a particular purpose. The advice and strategies contained herein may not be suitable for every situation.

ISBN: 978-1-7641942-1-1
Isohan Publishing

Table of Contents

Chapter 1: The Invisible Years

Walking through childhood feels like performing in a play where everyone else received the script except you. You watch other children navigate social situations with an ease that seems as natural as breathing, while you stand on the sidelines mentally cataloging their every gesture, their tone, their timing. The exhaustion begins early—not from running or playing, but from the constant work of translation. Every interaction requires you to decode unspoken rules that others seem to absorb through osmosis.

Growing Up Different but Not Knowing Why

The signs were always there, scattered like breadcrumbs through a childhood that looked normal from the outside but felt like walking through quicksand from within. Sarah, diagnosed at thirty-four, recalls her mother's frequent comment: "You're such an odd little duck." The words carried affection but also bewilderment. Sarah would spend hours arranging her toy horses by color and size, creating elaborate stories where each animal had specific personality traits based on their appearance. She could recite entire episodes of her favorite television shows verbatim but couldn't understand why her classmates didn't want to hear these performances during recess.

Research by Lai et al. (2015)[1] demonstrates that autism in girls often presents differently than in boys, leading to significant underdiagnosis. Girls tend to internalize their struggles rather than display disruptive behaviors, making their autism less visible to parents and teachers. They become masters of observation, studying their peers like anthropologists studying a foreign culture.

Consider Maria's experience growing up in a large Italian family. She learned to mirror her older sister's social behaviors so precisely that adults often praised her as "such a good girl" and "so well-behaved." What they didn't see was the hours she spent in her bedroom after family gatherings, physically and emotionally depleted from maintaining her performance. She developed elaborate rituals around

1

her belongings—books arranged by height, pencils sharpened to identical points, clothing folded in specific patterns. These routines provided comfort and control in a world that often felt chaotic and unpredictable.

The academic environment often masks autistic traits in intelligent girls. Teachers appreciate students who follow rules precisely, complete assignments thoroughly, and rarely cause disruptions. Emma excelled in school despite struggling to understand group projects and avoiding the cafeteria due to overwhelming sensory input. She ate lunch in the library every day, telling herself she preferred reading to socializing. The librarian, Mrs. Patterson, became a protective figure who allowed Emma to help organize books during lunch periods, providing structure and purpose while shielding her from social demands.

Masking, Mimicking, and the Exhaustion of Fitting In

The term "masking" describes the conscious or unconscious suppression of autistic traits to appear neurotypical. For many women, masking begins so early that distinguishing between their authentic self and their performed self becomes nearly impossible. The mask isn't just about behavior—it shapes thoughts, emotions, and even physical responses.

Gould and Ashton-Smith (2011)[2] found that girls with autism often develop sophisticated social mimicry skills, copying behaviors from peers, television characters, or books. This adaptation strategy allows them to navigate social situations but comes at significant personal cost. The energy required to maintain constant vigilance about appropriate responses leaves little room for authentic self-expression or emotional processing.

Jessica's story illustrates this phenomenon clearly. As a child, she would watch her popular classmate Jennifer with scientific precision, noting how Jennifer tilted her head during conversations, how she laughed at certain types of jokes, and how she positioned her body during group activities. Jessica created mental scripts for common

2

social scenarios, practicing responses in her bedroom mirror. "How was your weekend?" required specific types of answers—not too detailed, include one fun activity, ask the question back. She became so skilled at this performance that teachers and parents never suspected her struggles.

The physical toll of masking manifests in various ways. Many women report chronic fatigue, frequent headaches, and digestive issues throughout childhood and adolescence. Rachel, now thirty-eight, remembers coming home from school and immediately retreating to her room, claiming homework but actually needing hours to decompress from the day's social demands. She would rock in her chair or run her fingers repeatedly through her hair—self-soothing behaviors she instinctively hid from others.

Early Signs Missed by Family, Teachers, and Professionals

The medical and educational communities have historically based autism diagnostic criteria on research conducted primarily with boys. Attwood (2007)[3] notes that professionals often overlook autism in girls because their presentations don't match traditional expectations. Girls may appear socially engaged while actually following learned scripts, show intense interests in socially acceptable topics like horses or books, and direct their distress inward rather than outward.

Dr. Michelle Mowbray's case files reveal pattern after pattern of missed opportunities. Ten-year-old Anna was brought to therapy for "anxiety and perfectionism." She experienced meltdowns at home but never at school, leading therapists to focus on family dynamics rather than considering neurological differences. Anna's detailed drawings of fantasy worlds, her extensive knowledge of medieval history, and her difficulty with unstructured time were viewed as giftedness rather than potential autism indicators.

Parent observations often provide the clearest picture, yet these concerns are frequently dismissed. Linda brought her daughter Kate to three different pediatricians, describing Kate's extreme sensitivity to clothing textures, her distress over schedule changes, and her intense focus on specific topics. Each doctor reassured Linda that Kate was simply "bright and sensitive," missing the constellation of traits that clearly indicated autism.

Educational professionals, despite their training, often mistake autistic girls for having anxiety disorders, eating disorders, or attention difficulties. The subtle nature of female autism presentation means that obvious signs get reframed through neurotypical assumptions. Samantha's refusal to participate in group work was labeled as shyness rather than social communication differences. Her meticulous note-taking and perfect attendance masked her struggles with executive function and sensory processing.

The Cost of Camouflaging Autistic Traits

Living authentically requires enormous energy when your authentic self doesn't align with social expectations. Hull et al. (2017)[4] found that camouflaging autistic traits correlates with increased anxiety, depression, and suicidal ideation. The psychological cost accumulates over years, often leading to mental health crises in late adolescence or early adulthood.

The development of eating disorders among autistic girls represents one tragic consequence of masking pressure. Control over food intake can feel like the only area where precise rules and routines are socially acceptable. Madison's anorexia began during middle school when social demands intensified. Restricting food provided a sense of mastery and control while her eating disorder behaviors were praised as "discipline" and "self-control" by adults who didn't recognize her underlying autism.

Academic and career choices suffer when girls consistently prioritize fitting in over exploring genuine interests. Many women report abandoning subjects or activities they loved because they seemed "weird" or attracted unwanted attention. Patricia gave up her passion for entomology after classmates teased her extensive beetle collection. She shifted toward more socially acceptable interests, eventually choosing a college major based on what seemed normal rather than what engaged her mind.

The impact extends into relationship patterns as well. Learning to prioritize others' comfort over your own needs creates vulnerability to exploitation and abuse. Women who spend childhood suppressing their authentic responses often struggle to recognize manipulation or advocate for their boundaries in adult relationships.

Setting the Stage for Discovery

The invisible years create a foundation of confusion and self-doubt that persists into adulthood. Years of being told you're "too sensitive," "too particular," or "just anxious" can make you doubt your own perceptions and experiences. The constant message that your natural responses are wrong or inappropriate shapes self-concept in ways that require active healing later in life.

Yet these same years also develop remarkable strengths. The observational skills required for masking often translate into deep empathy and social awareness. The analytical approach to social interaction can lead to sophisticated understanding of human behavior. The persistence required to maintain camouflaging often develops into remarkable determination and resilience.

Understanding the invisible years provides context for everything that follows. The moment of autism recognition doesn't happen in isolation—it builds upon decades of accumulated experiences, missed opportunities, and unconscious adaptations. Recognizing these patterns allows women to approach their autism journey with both compassion for their younger selves and appreciation for the strength required to survive and thrive despite systemic misunderstanding.

The transition from invisibility to recognition represents a fundamental shift in self-understanding. After years of feeling like a puzzle piece forced into the wrong spaces, discovering autism offers the possibility of finding where you truly belong. The invisible years end not with dramatic revelation but with the gradual understanding that being different was never the problem—being unsupported and misunderstood was.

Key Insights from the Invisible Years

- Autistic girls often develop sophisticated masking skills that hide their struggles from adults
- Traditional autism criteria miss many girls because their presentations differ from male patterns
- The energy cost of constant camouflaging accumulates over time, leading to mental health challenges
- Early signs are frequently misinterpreted as giftedness, anxiety, or behavioral problems
- Understanding these patterns helps explain adult autism recognition and provides validation for past experiences

Chapter 2: The Awakening - Recognizing the Signs

The recognition moment rarely arrives like lightning. More often, it creeps in through side doors—a documentary watched by chance, an article shared by a friend, a conversation that shifts something fundamental in your understanding of yourself. The awakening to potential autism doesn't happen overnight but unfolds like a slow-motion revelation where pieces of a lifelong puzzle suddenly align into a picture that makes sense.

The Moment of Recognition: "This Might Be Me"

For thirty-two-year-old Jennifer, the moment came during a late-night internet session researching her daughter's behavioral challenges. As she read about autism in girls, each symptom description felt like reading her own biography. The echolalia she'd exhibited as a child, dismissed as "just being talkative." The intense friendships that burned brightly then ended abruptly when she couldn't maintain the social energy required. The way certain fabrics made her feel physically ill, explained away as "being picky."

The recognition experience varies dramatically among women, but common themes emerge. Many describe feeling simultaneously validated and overwhelmed. Years of self-blame and confusion suddenly have a potential explanation, but accepting this explanation means reframing an entire life story. The relief of understanding mixes with grief for missed opportunities and appropriate support.

Research by Lewis (2016)[5] indicates that women often identify potential autism through learning about their children's diagnoses or through media representation that accurately depicts female autism presentations. Social media platforms have become particularly powerful sources of recognition, where autistic women share experiences that resonate deeply with those still seeking answers.

Consider Sarah's experience discovering autism through a TikTok video about sensory processing differences. The creator described feeling overwhelmed in grocery stores, needing to wear specific clothing textures, and having physical reactions to certain sounds. Sarah had developed elaborate strategies to avoid fluorescent lighting and crowded spaces, never connecting these needs to a neurological difference. The video provided language for experiences she'd never been able to articulate.

The recognition moment often triggers intense research behaviors. Women describe consuming every available resource about autism, particularly information about late diagnosis and female presentations. This research serves multiple purposes: validating their suspicions, preparing for potential professional evaluation, and beginning to understand how autism might explain their life experiences.

Common Triggers for Self-Discovery in Adulthood

Several life circumstances commonly trigger autism recognition in women. Parenthood represents a significant catalyst, particularly when raising a child with obvious developmental differences. The process of learning about child development and neurological variations often leads parents to recognize similar patterns in their own histories.

Mental health crises frequently precede autism discovery. Jessica sought therapy for what she termed "chronic anxiety and social exhaustion" at age twenty-nine. Her therapist, Dr. Rodriguez, noticed that Jessica's anxiety seemed specifically tied to social and sensory situations rather than generalized worry. During their sessions, Jessica described detailed coping strategies she'd developed unconsciously— specific routes through buildings to avoid crowds, elaborate morning routines that couldn't be disrupted, and intense special interests that provided comfort and regulation.

Career transitions or academic challenges in adulthood can also spark recognition. Maria struggled through graduate school despite her intellectual capabilities, finding herself overwhelmed by group projects, oral presentations, and networking events that seemed effortless for her peers. Her academic advisor suggested she might benefit from disability services, leading her to research various conditions that might explain her specific pattern of strengths and challenges.

Relationship difficulties represent another common trigger. Many women seek couples therapy or individual counseling to address communication patterns they don't understand. The intensity of their emotions, their need for routine and predictability, and their communication style often conflict with neurotypical partners' expectations. Through therapy focused on understanding these differences, autism emerges as a potential explanation.

Burnout experiences frequently precede autism recognition, particularly among high-achieving women who have successfully masked throughout their careers. The accumulated stress of constant adaptation eventually overwhelms their coping systems. Dr. Amanda Kirby's research (2018)[6] found that autistic women often experience profound burnout in their thirties or forties, leading them to seek explanations for their sudden inability to function at previously manageable levels.

Researching Autism in Women and Late Diagnosis

Once potential autism recognition begins, women typically engage in extensive research to understand what this might mean for them. The research process serves both practical and emotional purposes— gathering information for potential professional evaluation while beginning to process the implications of late recognition.

The quality and accessibility of information about autism in women has improved dramatically in recent years, but significant gaps remain. Many clinical resources still reflect male-centered diagnostic criteria, leaving women to piece together information from academic papers, personal blogs, and social media accounts. Dr. Michelle Garnett's work (2019)[7] provides some of the most comprehensive clinical information about autism in women, helping bridge the gap between personal experience and professional understanding.

Online communities become particularly valuable during the research phase. Facebook groups, Reddit forums, and specialized websites offer spaces where women can ask questions, share experiences, and receive validation from others with similar stories. These communities provide information that clinical sources often miss— the daily reality of living as an autistic woman, strategies for managing sensory challenges, and scripts for discussing autism with family members or employers.

The research process often reveals how autism intersects with other aspects of identity. Women learn about masking and its psychological costs, understanding for the first time why social situations feel so draining. They discover information about sensory processing differences, executive function challenges, and the intense special interests that may have been dismissed or discouraged throughout their lives.

Kelly's research journey illustrates this process clearly. After recognizing potential autism at thirty-six, she spent months reading everything available about late diagnosis in women. She discovered that her childhood "obsessions" with specific animals, her need for detailed planning, and her difficulty with unstructured social time all aligned with autism presentations. More importantly, she learned that these traits weren't character flaws to overcome but neurological differences that could be accommodated and supported.

Fighting Imposter Syndrome and Self-Doubt

The period between recognition and potential diagnosis often involves intense self-doubt. Years of being told you're "too sensitive," "just anxious," or "perfectly normal" create internal voices that question the validity of autism considerations. Imposter syndrome becomes particularly acute when you've successfully masked autism traits, leading to thoughts like "I can't be autistic because I have friends" or "I can't be autistic because I did well in school."

Understanding masking becomes crucial for overcoming these doubts. Women learn that their ability to appear neurotypical doesn't negate their autism—it demonstrates the sophisticated adaptation skills they developed to survive in a neurotypical world. The cost of this masking, including chronic exhaustion, anxiety, and identity confusion, provides evidence supporting rather than contradicting autism considerations.

Professional skepticism can reinforce self-doubt. Many healthcare providers lack training in autism presentations in women, leading them to dismiss or minimize women's concerns. Rebecca's family doctor told her that she "seemed too social" to be autistic, not understanding that her social skills were consciously learned rather than intuitive. These professional responses can trigger shame and self-questioning, particularly for women already vulnerable to doubting their own perceptions.

The comparison trap represents another significant challenge. Women may compare themselves to stereotypical autism presentations or to other autistic individuals, concluding they're "not autistic enough" to warrant consideration. This thinking reflects internalized ableism and misunderstanding about autism as a spectrum condition with diverse presentations.

Support from other late-diagnosed women becomes invaluable during this phase. Hearing stories from women with similar experiences provides validation and perspective. Online communities often include specific support for women questioning potential autism, offering guidance for navigating self-doubt and preparing for professional evaluation.

Building Courage for Formal Assessment

The decision to pursue formal assessment requires considerable courage, particularly for women who have learned to minimize their own needs and experiences. The assessment process involves vulnerability—sharing childhood memories, discussing current challenges, and risking professional dismissal or invalidation.

Financial considerations often complicate assessment decisions. Adult autism evaluations can cost thousands of dollars and are rarely covered by insurance. Many women must weigh the potential benefits of formal diagnosis against significant financial investment, particularly if they're already supporting children with special needs or managing other medical expenses.

The fear of being wrong creates another barrier. Women worry about "wasting" professionals' time or resources if their suspicions prove unfounded. This concern reflects both genuine anxiety and internalized messages about not deserving attention or support. Learning that questioning potential autism is always valid—regardless of eventual outcomes—helps women move forward with assessment plans.

Practical preparation for assessment involves gathering documentation from childhood, identifying current challenges, and researching qualified evaluators. Many women create detailed timelines of their developmental history, collect school records, and reach out to family members for additional perspective. This preparation serves both practical and emotional purposes, helping them feel more confident about the assessment process.

The decision to pursue assessment often represents a fundamental shift in self-advocacy. For women accustomed to minimizing their needs, actively seeking professional evaluation requires developing new skills around recognizing and communicating their experiences. This growth often continues throughout the diagnosis process and beyond, becoming a foundation for ongoing self-advocacy in various life areas.

Reflections on Recognition

The awakening phase sets the stage for everything that follows in the autism journey. Recognition provides the first glimpse of an alternative explanation for lifelong experiences, but it also raises numerous questions about identity, relationships, and future directions. Understanding this phase as a process rather than a single moment helps women navigate the complexity of potential late autism diagnosis with patience and self-compassion.

The courage required to consider autism, research thoroughly, and pursue assessment demonstrates remarkable strength and self-awareness. Women who reach this point have already begun the important work of understanding and advocating for themselves, regardless of eventual diagnosis outcomes.

Key Insights from the Awakening

- Recognition often occurs through learning about children's diagnoses or encountering accurate media representation
- The research phase serves both informational and emotional processing purposes
- Self-doubt is normal and often reflects years of being told your experiences aren't valid
- Online communities provide crucial support and information during the recognition process
- Pursuing assessment requires courage and represents an important step in self-advocacy development

Chapter 3: Seeking Diagnosis

The path from autism recognition to formal diagnosis resembles navigating a medical system designed for a different population entirely. Most diagnostic protocols were developed based on research with autistic boys, leaving adult women to advocate for assessment approaches that recognize their unique presentations. The professional journey requires persistence, self-advocacy skills, and often considerable financial resources—all while managing the emotional complexity of potentially reframing your entire life story.

Finding Autism-Informed Professionals

Locating qualified professionals represents the first major challenge in seeking adult autism diagnosis. Many psychologists and psychiatrists receive minimal training in autism presentations, particularly in women and adults. The professional directory search becomes a research project in itself, requiring careful evaluation of providers' experience, training, and approach to autism assessment.

Dr. Sarah Johnson's clinic in Portland, Oregon, exemplifies the specialized expertise needed for accurate adult autism assessment. Dr. Johnson completed additional training in adult autism diagnosis and regularly attends conferences focused on autism in women. Her assessment protocol includes specific tools designed for adult populations and incorporates understanding of masking and camouflaging behaviors. Patients travel from across the Pacific Northwest to access her services, highlighting the scarcity of truly qualified providers.

Professional credentials alone don't guarantee appropriate expertise. Many licensed psychologists have limited experience with autism assessment, particularly for adults. Women often discover this gap only after scheduling appointments, making it essential to ask specific questions during initial consultations. Does the provider use assessment tools normed for adults? Do they understand masking in women? How many adult women have they diagnosed with autism?

Geographic location significantly impacts access to qualified providers. Rural areas often lack any professionals with autism assessment experience, forcing women to travel considerable distances or settle for inadequate evaluations. Telehealth options have expanded somewhat during recent years, but many assessment components require in-person administration.

Insurance networks further complicate provider selection. Many autism specialists don't accept insurance, requiring patients to pay out-of-pocket and potentially seek reimbursement later. This financial barrier prevents many women from accessing appropriate assessment, particularly those from lower socioeconomic backgrounds who may benefit most from diagnosis and support services.

The search process often relies heavily on community recommendations. Online forums, social media groups, and local autism organizations provide valuable information about provider quality and approach. Women share detailed reviews of their assessment experiences, warning others about dismissive providers while recommending those who demonstrate genuine understanding of female autism presentations.

The Assessment Process for Adults

Adult autism assessment differs significantly from childhood evaluation protocols. Developmental history becomes paramount, requiring detailed information about early childhood behaviors that may have been dismissed or normalized at the time. Many women find themselves contacting family members, searching for school records, and reconstructing memories from decades past.

The Autism Diagnostic Observation Schedule (ADOS-2) remains a cornerstone of autism assessment, but its limitations with masked adults are well-documented. Lai et al. (2017)[8] found that women who have developed sophisticated masking skills may not display obvious autism traits during structured assessment situations. Skilled evaluators supplement standardized tools with detailed clinical interviews and observational data from multiple sources.

Rachel's assessment experience illustrates both the potential and limitations of current protocols. During her ADOS-2 administration, she appeared socially engaged and appropriately responsive. However, her detailed self-report revealed the enormous effort required to maintain this presentation and the exhaustion that followed social interactions. Her evaluator, Dr. Martinez, recognized these patterns and weighted the self-report heavily in her diagnostic decision-making.

Comprehensive adult autism assessment typically spans multiple sessions and includes several components. Clinical interviews explore developmental history, current functioning, and specific autism-related behaviors. Cognitive testing may identify learning differences or intellectual abilities that influence autism presentation. Sensory processing evaluations can reveal patterns that support autism diagnosis even when social communication differences are subtle.

The assessment process often triggers intense emotions and memories. Women may recall childhood experiences they had forgotten or reframe previously confusing events through an autism lens. This emotional processing can feel overwhelming, particularly for those who have spent years attributing their struggles to personal failings rather than neurological differences.

Family involvement in assessment varies widely depending on individual circumstances. Some women bring partners or parents to provide additional perspective on their functioning. Others prefer to navigate the process independently, particularly if family members are skeptical about autism considerations or lack understanding of female presentations.

Navigating Healthcare Bias and Misconceptions

Healthcare providers often carry unconscious biases about autism that can interfere with accurate assessment. The stereotype of autism as a childhood condition affecting primarily boys leads some professionals to dismiss adult women's concerns outright. Dr. Lisa Croen's research (2019)[9] documents significant gender and age bias in autism diagnosis, with women facing longer delays and more skepticism from healthcare providers.

Common misconceptions about autism can derail the assessment process before it begins. Providers may assume that women with college degrees, successful careers, or romantic relationships cannot be autistic. These assumptions reflect fundamental misunderstanding of autism as a neurological difference rather than a deficit condition.

The "you seem too social" response represents one of the most frequent dismissals women encounter. Providers who lack training in masking behaviors may interpret learned social skills as evidence against autism diagnosis. Women often need to educate their evaluators about the difference between intuitive social understanding and consciously acquired social performance.

Professional training programs rarely include adequate education about autism in women and adults. Medical schools and psychology doctoral programs may devote minimal time to autism topics, focusing primarily on childhood presentations when they do. This training gap means that even well-intentioned providers may lack the knowledge needed for accurate assessment.

Advocating for appropriate assessment often requires considerable assertiveness. Women may need to request specific providers, insist on comprehensive evaluation, or seek second opinions when initial assessments are inadequate. This self-advocacy can feel particularly challenging for individuals who have learned to minimize their needs or defer to authority figures.

Cultural and racial bias adds additional complexity to the assessment process. Autism research and diagnostic tools have been developed primarily with white, middle-class populations. Women from diverse backgrounds may face additional skepticism or may have autism presentations that don't align with culturally narrow expectations.

Cost Considerations and Insurance Challenges

The financial burden of adult autism assessment often exceeds thousands of dollars, creating significant barriers for many women seeking diagnosis. Comprehensive evaluations typically cost between $2,000 and $5,000, depending on geographic location and provider experience. These costs often must be paid upfront, even when insurance plans theoretically cover autism assessment.

Insurance coverage for adult autism diagnosis remains inconsistent and often inadequate. Many plans cover autism assessment only for children or require extensive pre-authorization processes that can delay evaluation for months. Even when coverage exists, networks may lack qualified providers, forcing women to seek out-of-network services at higher personal cost.

The lack of standardized billing codes for adult autism assessment complicates insurance reimbursement. Providers may need to use general psychological evaluation codes that don't accurately reflect the specialized nature of autism assessment. This coding mismatch can lead to claim denials or reduced reimbursement rates.

Some women choose to pursue assessment through public health systems or university training clinics to reduce costs. These options may provide adequate evaluation at lower fees, but often involve longer waiting periods and may lack the specialized expertise needed for accurate adult female autism assessment.

Financial assistance programs exist but are limited in scope and availability. Some nonprofit organizations offer grants for autism assessment, particularly for individuals from underserved communities. However, these resources rarely meet demand, leaving many women unable to access formal diagnosis despite strong clinical indicators.

The cost-benefit analysis of pursuing formal diagnosis becomes particularly complex for women who have developed effective coping strategies independently. Some choose to forgo formal assessment while still embracing autism identity and accessing community support. Others view official diagnosis as essential for workplace accommodations, healthcare advocacy, or family understanding.

Preparing for the Evaluation Appointment

Thorough preparation can significantly improve the quality and accuracy of autism assessment. Women often spend weeks or months gathering documentation, organizing their thoughts, and preparing for the emotional intensity of the evaluation process. This preparation serves both practical and psychological purposes, helping ensure comprehensive assessment while building confidence for self-advocacy.

Creating a detailed developmental timeline helps evaluators understand autism traits that may have been missed or misinterpreted during childhood. This timeline should include information about early language development, social behaviors, sensory sensitivities, and special interests. Family photos and videos can provide valuable observational data about childhood functioning.

School records often contain relevant information about academic performance, social behaviors, and teacher observations. Report cards, individualized education programs, and disciplinary records can reveal patterns consistent with autism even when explicit concerns weren't raised at the time. Many women request these records months in advance, as schools may require time to locate historical documentation.

Preparing specific examples of current autism-related challenges helps evaluators understand adult functioning patterns. Women often create lists of sensory sensitivities, social communication difficulties, executive function challenges, and coping strategies they've developed. Specific examples carry more weight than general descriptions during clinical interviews.

Understanding assessment tools and procedures reduces anxiety and helps women participate more effectively in the evaluation process. Learning about the ADOS-2, clinical interviews, and cognitive testing components allows for more informed participation and better self-advocacy during the assessment.

Emotional preparation for assessment involves acknowledging the potential outcomes and their implications. Some women may receive autism diagnoses that validate their experiences and provide access to support services. Others may not meet diagnostic criteria despite experiencing autism-related challenges. Preparing for both possibilities helps manage expectations and reduces assessment-related stress.

Moving Forward with Knowledge

The professional journey toward autism diagnosis requires navigation of systemic barriers, financial challenges, and professional bias. Success often depends on persistence, self-advocacy skills, and access to resources that many women lack. Understanding these challenges helps normalize the difficulty of seeking assessment while highlighting the importance of systemic changes to improve access and quality of autism evaluation services.

Regardless of assessment outcomes, the process of seeking diagnosis often provides valuable self-knowledge and validation. Women learn to articulate their experiences, advocate for their needs, and connect with communities of support. These skills prove valuable throughout life, extending far beyond the specific question of autism diagnosis.

Key Insights from the Professional Journey

- Finding qualified providers requires extensive research and often involves geographic and financial barriers
- Assessment protocols designed for children may miss autism presentations in masked adults
- Healthcare bias and misconceptions can interfere with accurate evaluation and appropriate support
- Insurance coverage remains inadequate and inconsistent for adult autism assessment
- Thorough preparation improves assessment quality and helps women advocate effectively for their needs

Chapter 4: The Diagnosis Day

The moment of receiving an autism diagnosis carries weight that extends far beyond clinical terminology. Years of searching for explanations, questioning your own perceptions, and navigating a world that never quite fit suddenly crystallize into a single conversation with a professional who validates what you've suspected. Yet the emotions that follow rarely align with simple relief or straightforward acceptance. Instead, diagnosis day often initiates a complex grief process that encompasses loss, validation, anger, and hope in measures that shift like sand.

Receiving the Official Diagnosis

The actual delivery of autism diagnosis varies dramatically depending on the provider's communication style and understanding of the implications for adult women. Some professionals approach the conversation with clinical detachment, presenting results as factual information without acknowledging the emotional significance. Others recognize the profound impact of late diagnosis and create space for processing the complex feelings that arise.

Dr. Patricia Williams, a psychologist specializing in adult autism assessment, describes her approach to diagnosis delivery: "I always begin by asking what the person hopes to gain from this evaluation. Understanding their goals helps me frame the results in ways that feel supportive rather than pathological." Her patients often express surprise at being asked about their perspective, having expected a more authoritative, one-way delivery of information.

Jennifer's diagnosis experience illustrates the power of thoughtful delivery. After completing her comprehensive assessment, Dr. Williams began their results session by saying, "The testing confirms what you suspected—you are autistic. This explains many of the experiences you've described throughout your life." The validation felt immediate and profound. Jennifer later reflected, "Hearing 'this explains' rather than 'you have a disorder' completely changed how I received the information."

Not all diagnosis experiences provide such affirmation. Maria received her results through a brief phone call from a provider who seemed rushed and uncomfortable. "The testing indicates autism spectrum disorder," the psychologist stated matter-of-factly. "We'll send you a report with recommendations." The clinical tone and lack of discussion left Maria feeling more confused than validated, unsure what autism diagnosis meant for her daily life or future plans.

The diagnostic report itself often becomes a treasured document— concrete proof that your experiences have been acknowledged and validated by a professional. Many women describe reading their reports multiple times, particularly sections that describe childhood behaviors or current challenges they've never been able to articulate clearly. These reports provide language for experiences that previously lacked names.

The timing of diagnosis delivery can significantly impact the emotional response. Some women prefer immediate results when possible, wanting to process information while still in the clinical setting with professional support available. Others need time to prepare emotionally and prefer scheduled follow-up appointments specifically focused on discussing results and implications.

Complex Emotions: Validation vs. Grief

The emotional response to autism diagnosis defies simple categorization. Relief at finally having an explanation often mingles with grief over missed opportunities and years of struggle without support. Validation of your experiences coexists with anger at systems that failed to recognize your needs earlier. These seemingly contradictory emotions can leave women feeling confused about how they "should" feel about their diagnosis.

Research by Crane et al. (2018)[10] found that late autism diagnosis often triggers what psychologists term "complicated grief"— mourning for a different life path while simultaneously celebrating increased self-understanding. This grief process doesn't follow predictable stages but rather cycles through various emotions as women integrate their new identity and understanding.

The validation component of diagnosis brings profound relief to many women. After years of being told they're "too sensitive," "just anxious," or "perfectly normal," professional confirmation that their experiences reflect real neurological differences can feel revolutionary. Susan, diagnosed at forty-one, described this validation: "For the first time in my life, someone was telling me that my struggles were real and had a name. I wasn't defective or failing— I was autistic."

Yet validation often coexists with grief for the child who struggled without understanding or support. Women frequently mourn the years spent believing they were somehow fundamentally flawed rather than neurologically different. This grief extends to educational opportunities missed, relationships damaged by misunderstanding, and career paths abandoned due to unsupported challenges.

Anger represents another common emotional response, particularly toward systems and individuals who dismissed concerns or provided inadequate support. Parents who insisted "you're fine, just try harder" become targets of resentment, as do teachers who punished autistic behaviors rather than providing accommodation. Healthcare providers who minimized concerns or provided incorrect diagnoses may also become focal points for processing anger about delayed recognition.

The complexity of these emotions can feel overwhelming, particularly for women who have learned to suppress or ignore their emotional responses. The intensity of feelings following diagnosis often surprises women who expected simple relief or acceptance. Understanding that complex emotional responses are normal and healthy becomes crucial for processing the diagnosis experience.

Reframing Your Entire Life Story

Autism diagnosis necessitates a complete reconstruction of personal narrative. Events that previously felt shameful or confusing suddenly make sense when viewed through an autism lens. The social difficulties that seemed like personal failures become recognized as neurological differences requiring accommodation rather than correction. This reframing process can take months or years to complete fully.

Childhood experiences often require the most significant reframing. The little girl who spent recess alone reading wasn't antisocial—she was managing sensory overwhelm and finding comfort in special interests. The teenager who struggled with group projects wasn't lazy or uncooperative—she was experiencing executive function challenges and social communication differences that nobody recognized or supported.

Academic experiences frequently take on new meaning after diagnosis. Rachel, diagnosed at thirty-eight, realized that her college struggles weren't due to inadequate intelligence or poor study habits. Her difficulty with group discussions, sensitivity to classroom lighting, and need for detailed syllabi all reflected autism-related challenges that could have been accommodated with appropriate support.

Career patterns often make more sense when viewed through an autism lens. Many women recognize that their job satisfaction correlates strongly with autism-friendly features: clear expectations, minimal social demands, opportunity to use special interests, and sensory-appropriate environments. Understanding these patterns helps explain career successes and struggles while informing future professional decisions.

Relationship history requires particularly sensitive reframing. Many women realize that their relationship challenges stemmed from neurological differences in communication style, sensory needs, and emotional processing rather than character flaws or inadequate effort. This understanding can improve current relationships while helping process grief about past relationship difficulties.

The reframing process isn't always positive. Some women struggle with regret about missed opportunities or anger about unsupported struggles. These feelings are valid and important parts of processing late diagnosis. Working with autism-informed therapists can help navigate the complex emotions that arise during life story reconstruction.

Sharing the News with Important People

The decision about disclosure involves careful consideration of relationships, timing, and potential consequences. Not everyone in your life needs to know about your autism diagnosis, and you maintain complete control over who receives this information and how it's presented. The disclosure process often becomes an opportunity to educate others about autism while setting new boundaries around understanding and support.

Family disclosure often proves most complex due to long-standing relationship dynamics and potential defensive responses. Parents may feel guilty about missing autism signs or resistant to accepting that their parenting didn't cause your struggles. Siblings might question why they didn't receive similar attention or wonder about their own neurological differences. These responses, while sometimes painful, often reflect family members' own processing of new information rather than rejection of your experience.

Partner disclosure frequently strengthens relationships by providing framework for understanding communication differences and sensory needs. Many partners report feeling relieved to learn that relationship challenges stemmed from neurological differences rather than lack of caring or effort. This understanding often leads to improved accommodation and communication strategies.

Close friends may respond with validation and support, particularly if they've observed your struggles firsthand. Some friends become autism advocates and allies, educating themselves about autism and adjusting their expectations and interactions accordingly. Others may struggle to understand or accept the diagnosis, particularly if they've internalized stereotypes about autism.

Professional disclosure requires careful strategic thinking about potential benefits and risks. Workplace protections exist for disclosed disabilities, but discrimination persists despite legal protections. Some women choose to disclose for accommodation purposes, while others prefer to maintain privacy while independently managing their autism-related needs.

The language used for disclosure can significantly impact others' responses. Presenting autism as a neurological difference rather than a disorder often elicits more positive reactions. Emphasizing how autism explains your experiences rather than focusing on deficits helps others understand the information constructively.

Beginning the Integration Process

Integration of autism identity begins immediately after diagnosis but continues throughout life as understanding deepens and circumstances change. This process involves both internal work around self-acceptance and external changes in how you navigate the world with new self-knowledge. Integration success often depends on accessing appropriate support resources and connecting with autism communities.

The initial integration period frequently involves intensive learning about autism, particularly female presentations and adult manifestations. Many women describe reading everything available about autism while connecting with online communities for validation and practical guidance. This research phase serves both educational and emotional purposes, helping develop autism identity while building knowledge for self-advocacy.

Practical integration involves identifying accommodation needs and developing strategies for implementing them. Understanding your sensory profile helps explain environmental preferences and aversions. Recognizing executive function patterns explains organizational challenges while suggesting helpful tools and strategies. This practical application of autism knowledge often provides immediate improvement in daily functioning.

Social integration requires developing new scripts and expectations for relationships. Learning to advocate for your needs, set appropriate boundaries, and communicate your autism-related requirements becomes an ongoing process. Some relationships strengthen through increased understanding, while others may need to change or end if accommodation isn't possible.

The integration process often involves grief work around lost opportunities and delayed understanding. Working with autism-informed therapists can help process these complex emotions while developing strategies for moving forward. Many women find that individual therapy combined with autism-specific support groups provides the most comprehensive support during integration.

Professional integration may involve career changes, accommodation requests, or educational pursuits that better align with autism strengths and interests. Some women return to school to study autism or helping professions, while others make career changes that provide better sensory environments or utilize their special interests more directly.

Thoughts on New Beginnings

Diagnosis day marks the end of one chapter while opening another filled with possibility and challenge. The complexity of emotions surrounding late autism diagnosis reflects the significance of this life change and the years of struggle that preceded recognition. Understanding that mixed feelings are normal and healthy helps women navigate this transition with self-compassion and realistic expectations.

The integration process following diagnosis extends far beyond the clinical appointment, becoming a lifelong journey of self-discovery and advocacy. While the path isn't always smooth, most women report that autism diagnosis ultimately improves their quality of life by providing understanding, community, and tools for effective self-advocacy.

Key Insights from Diagnosis Day

- Emotional responses to diagnosis are typically complex, involving validation, grief, anger, and relief simultaneously
- Life story reframing takes time and often reveals patterns that make sense for the first time
- Disclosure decisions should be strategic and based on potential benefits and risks in each relationship
- Integration is an ongoing process requiring both internal work and external accommodation
- Professional support during the integration period can significantly improve outcomes and emotional adjustment

Chapter 5: Unmasking

The journey from autism diagnosis to authentic living requires dismantling years of carefully constructed social camouflage. Unmasking represents one of the most challenging yet liberating aspects of late autism diagnosis—gradually releasing the exhausting performance of neurotypicality while discovering who you truly are beneath layers of learned behaviors. This process isn't simply about stopping pretense; it's about archaeological work to uncover interests, needs, and expressions that have been buried under decades of adaptation.

Understanding Masking and Its Effects

Masking, also termed camouflaging, involves conscious and unconscious suppression of autistic traits to appear neurotypical. Research by Hull et al. (2019)[11] demonstrates that masking behaviors begin early in childhood and often become so automatic that distinguishing between authentic self and performed self becomes nearly impossible. For women, masking typically involves sophisticated social mimicry, emotional suppression, and exhausting hypervigilance about appropriate responses.

The neurological cost of chronic masking extends far beyond simple fatigue. Constant monitoring of behavior, suppression of natural responses, and performance of learned social scripts requires enormous cognitive resources. Dr. Michelle Mowbray's longitudinal study (2020)[12] found that women who engaged in extensive masking throughout childhood and adolescence showed significantly higher rates of anxiety, depression, and burnout in adulthood compared to those who had received early autism recognition and support.

Understanding masking involves recognizing both obvious and subtle forms of camouflaging behavior. Obvious masking includes forcing eye contact during conversations, suppressing stimming behaviors in public, and following social scripts for small talk despite finding these interactions meaningless. Subtle masking encompasses choosing clothing based on social appropriateness rather than sensory comfort, agreeing to social activities that drain your energy, and modulating your voice to match others' expectations.

The development of masking behaviors often begins so early that women struggle to identify which behaviors represent their authentic selves versus learned performance. Sarah, diagnosed at thirty-four, spent months observing her own behavior with new awareness. She realized that her animated storytelling style, which she'd always considered natural, was actually mimicry of a charismatic teacher from elementary school. Her genuine communication style was more reserved and precise, requiring significantly less energy to maintain.

Physical masking behaviors often persist long after conscious masking decisions end. Years of suppressing stimming can leave women disconnected from their natural self-regulation mechanisms. Forcing uncomfortable eye contact can create lasting anxiety around visual attention during conversations. These physical patterns require intentional unlearning and replacement with more authentic responses.

The psychological impact of chronic masking includes identity confusion, difficulty accessing emotions, and challenges with self-advocacy. When your authentic responses have been consistently suppressed, knowing what you actually think, feel, or need becomes genuinely difficult. Many women describe feeling like actresses who've been playing the same role so long they've forgotten their original character.

Gradual Unmasking Strategies

Unmasking requires a gradual, strategic approach rather than sudden abandonment of all learned behaviors. Decades of masking can't be undone overnight, and sudden dramatic changes in behavior can shock family members, colleagues, and friends who have never seen your authentic self. Successful unmasking involves careful selection of environments and relationships where authentic expression feels safe and supported.

The concept of "unmasking practice areas" helps women begin this process safely. These might include your bedroom, your car during commutes, or time spent with autism-affirming friends who understand and support your authentic expression. Starting with small authenticity experiments in low-stakes situations builds confidence for larger changes while providing data about which authentic behaviors feel most important to maintain.

Physical environment modifications often represent early unmasking steps. Allowing yourself to wear headphones in public, choosing restaurants based on lighting and noise levels rather than social expectations, or creating sensory-friendly spaces in your home demonstrates self-advocacy while providing immediate relief from masking demands. These environmental changes require minimal explanation to others while significantly reducing daily masking pressure.

Communication unmasking involves gradually reducing forced social behaviors while developing more authentic interaction styles. This might mean allowing natural pauses in conversation rather than filling silence with meaningless chatter, expressing genuine interests instead of discussing socially expected topics, or reducing forced emotional expression to match your actual feelings rather than others' expectations.

Workplace unmasking requires particular care due to potential professional consequences. Starting with small accommodations like requesting written instructions rather than verbal directions, using noise-canceling headphones, or taking breaks in quiet spaces can improve functioning without requiring extensive disclosure. These changes often improve work performance while reducing the energy cost of professional masking.

Relationship unmasking involves honest conversations with family members and friends about your autism diagnosis and changing needs. This process often strengthens genuine relationships while revealing which connections were based primarily on your masked persona rather than authentic compatibility. Some relationships may need to change or end if accommodation isn't possible, while others deepen through increased honesty and understanding.

Rediscovering Suppressed Interests and Stims

Years of masking often involve abandoning special interests that seemed "weird" or age-inappropriate while suppressing stimming behaviors that provided regulation and comfort. Unmasking includes permission to reconnect with these authentic aspects of yourself, even if they don't align with neurotypical expectations for adult women.

Special interests frequently represent some of the most suppressed aspects of masked identity. Many women abandoned passionate interests during adolescence due to social pressure or teasing. Reconnecting with these interests often provides immediate joy and sense of authentic self-expression. Jennifer, diagnosed at thirty-six, had loved collecting and studying insects as a child but abandoned this interest in middle school after classmates called it "gross." Post-diagnosis, she returned to entomology with adult resources and perspective, eventually turning her interest into a successful science communication blog.

The process of rediscovering interests often involves giving yourself permission to explore topics deeply without justification or practical application. Autism-friendly interests might include detailed knowledge about specific historical periods, comprehensive understanding of particular animal species, or extensive collection and categorization of items that bring joy. These interests provide regulation, comfort, and genuine engagement that masked activities rarely achieve.

Stimming behaviors require careful reintroduction due to years of suppression and potential social stigma. Many women discover that they've unconsciously replaced obvious stims with more socially acceptable repetitive behaviors—twirling hair instead of hand-flapping, tapping feet instead of rocking, or clicking pens instead of vocal stimming. Reconnecting with natural stimming often improves emotional regulation while reducing anxiety and overwhelm.

The social acceptability of various stims influences reintroduction strategies. Some stimming behaviors, like fidgeting with jewelry or tapping fingers, blend relatively well with neurotypical environments. Others, like vocal stimming or full-body rocking, may require privacy or specifically autism-friendly environments. The goal isn't to stim constantly in all environments but to have access to effective self-regulation when needed.

Creating "stim kits" for different environments helps support authentic self-regulation while managing social considerations. A workplace stim kit might include subtle fidget tools, textured objects for tactile stimming, or noise-canceling headphones for auditory regulation. Home stim kits can include more obvious tools like weighted blankets, spinning toys, or items specifically chosen for their sensory properties.

Sensory Awareness and Accommodation

Unmasking often reveals sensory experiences that have been minimized or ignored during years of forced accommodation to neurotypical environments. Developing sensory awareness involves paying attention to your authentic responses to various inputs while learning to advocate for environments that support rather than challenge your sensory system.

Sensory profiles vary dramatically among autistic individuals, making self-discovery essential for effective accommodation. Some women discover they're hypersensitive to specific sounds, lights, or textures that they've been tolerating at significant personal cost. Others find they're hyposensitive and need more intense sensory input for effective regulation. Understanding your unique profile enables targeted accommodation strategies.

Auditory sensitivity often represents one of the most challenging sensory differences to accommodate in neurotypical environments. Background conversations, fluorescent light buzzing, or unexpected sounds can create significant distress and interference with concentration. Developing awareness of your auditory triggers enables strategic use of noise-canceling headphones, choice of seating in restaurants, and advocacy for quieter work environments.

Visual sensitivity encompasses both lighting issues and visual processing challenges. Fluorescent lights, flashing screens, or busy visual environments can cause headaches, fatigue, and concentration difficulties. Some women discover that sunglasses indoors, specific lighting choices, or modified computer screen settings dramatically improve their comfort and functioning.

Tactile sensitivity affects clothing choices, physical contact preferences, and environmental comfort. Years of wearing uncomfortable clothing to appear professional or fashionable may have created chronic stress without conscious awareness. Unmasking often involves wardrobe changes that prioritize sensory comfort while still meeting social or professional requirements.

Developing sensory accommodation strategies requires both self-awareness and environmental modification skills. This might involve carrying sensory tools like fidgets or noise-reducing headphones, modifying home environments for optimal comfort, or advocating for workplace accommodations that address sensory challenges.

Building Authentic Self-Expression

Authentic self-expression extends beyond behavior modification to encompass communication style, emotional expression, and life choices that align with your genuine preferences rather than social expectations. This process often involves unlearning years of performed responses while developing confidence in your natural communication and expression patterns.

Communication style unmasking frequently reveals more direct, precise language patterns than typical social conversation. Many autistic women naturally prefer specific, factual communication over small talk or emotional implications. Allowing yourself to communicate authentically often improves relationship quality while reducing the exhausting work of translation between your thoughts and socially expected responses.

Emotional expression authenticity involves connecting with your genuine emotional responses rather than performing expected feelings. Years of masking often include emotional camouflaging—smiling when frustrated, expressing enthusiasm for activities you dislike, or minimizing distress to avoid burdening others. Authentic emotional expression requires learning to identify and communicate your actual feelings.

Life choice authenticity encompasses career decisions, relationship patterns, and lifestyle preferences that align with your autism-related needs and interests. This might involve career changes that better accommodate sensory sensitivities, relationship structures that honor your need for routine and predictability, or social choices that prioritize quality over quantity in friendships.

Creative expression often flourishes during unmasking as suppressed interests and authentic perspectives emerge. Many women discover artistic, writing, or creative abilities that were discouraged or abandoned during their masking years. Autism-related attention to detail, pattern recognition, and unique perspectives often translate into distinctive creative voices.

The process of building authentic self-expression requires patience and self-compassion. Years of masking can't be undone quickly, and the journey toward authenticity involves both progress and setbacks. Celebrating small steps toward authentic living while maintaining realistic expectations for the timeline helps sustain motivation during challenging periods.

Reflections on Authentic Living

Unmasking represents both an ending and a beginning—the end of exhausting performance and the beginning of authentic self-discovery. This process requires courage, patience, and often significant life changes as you align your external circumstances with your internal reality. While challenging, unmasking typically leads to improved mental health, stronger relationships, and greater life satisfaction as the energy previously devoted to camouflaging becomes available for more meaningful pursuits.

The journey toward authentic self-expression benefits from community support, professional guidance, and realistic expectations for the timeline and process. Each step toward authenticity, no matter how small, represents progress toward a life that honors your genuine needs, interests, and expressions.

Key Insights from Unmasking

- Masking behaviors often become so automatic that identifying authentic responses requires conscious observation and practice
- Gradual unmasking in safe environments builds confidence for larger authenticity steps
- Rediscovering suppressed interests and stims often provides immediate improvement in emotional regulation and life satisfaction
- Sensory awareness and accommodation dramatically improve daily functioning and comfort
- Authentic self-expression encompasses communication style, emotional responses, and life choices that align with genuine preferences

Chapter 6: Relationships Reimagined

The revelation of autism diagnosis sends ripples through every existing relationship, requiring renegotiation of expectations, boundaries, and communication patterns that may have been established over decades. Family members and friends who thought they knew you discover they've been interacting with a carefully constructed persona rather than your authentic self. This recognition can strengthen relationships through increased understanding or expose fundamental incompatibilities that were previously masked by your accommodation efforts.

Explaining Autism to Loved Ones

The conversation about autism diagnosis often represents the first time many family members encounter accurate information about autism, particularly female presentations. Years of media misrepresentation and outdated stereotypes create preconceptions that can interfere with understanding your specific experiences. Successful autism disclosure requires both education about autism generally and specific explanation of how autism manifests in your life.

Educational preparation becomes essential before disclosure conversations. Many women create simple handouts or resource lists that explain autism in women, late diagnosis, and masking behaviors. Dr. Sarah Hendrickx's materials (2020)[13] specifically address family education needs, providing clear explanations of autism characteristics without pathological language that might alarm or alienate family members.

The timing and setting of disclosure conversations significantly impact their reception. Choosing calm, private moments when family members can process information without distraction improves the likelihood of productive discussion. Some women prefer one-on-one conversations that allow for individual processing, while others choose family meetings that ensure consistent information sharing.

Jennifer's disclosure experience with her parents illustrates both potential challenges and rewards of family education. Initially, her mother responded with guilt and self-blame: "How did we miss this? What did we do wrong?" Her father questioned the diagnosis validity: "You seem fine to us. Are you sure this doctor knows what they're talking about?" These responses, while painful, reflected their limited understanding of autism rather than rejection of Jennifer's experience.

The conversation shifted when Jennifer provided specific examples of childhood behaviors that made sense through an autism lens. Her intense interest in horses, her distress over clothing textures, and her need for predictable routines suddenly aligned into a recognizable pattern. Her parents began connecting dots they hadn't previously understood, leading to validation and increased support.

Language choice during disclosure conversations influences family responses significantly. Presenting autism as a neurological difference rather than a disorder reduces stigma and defensiveness. Emphasizing how autism explains your experiences rather than focusing on deficits helps family members understand diagnosis as clarification rather than catastrophe.

Providing concrete examples of how autism affects your daily life helps family members understand practical implications. Explaining sensory sensitivities, social exhaustion, or executive function challenges gives family members specific information they can use to improve interactions and provide appropriate support.

Renegotiating Relationship Expectations

Autism diagnosis often reveals that relationship dynamics have been shaped by your unconscious accommodation and masking rather than genuine compatibility or mutual understanding. Family members may need to adjust expectations about social participation, emotional expression, and communication styles that have been based on your performed rather than authentic responses.

Holiday and family gathering traditions frequently require renegotiation after autism diagnosis. Events that previously felt stressful but manageable may need modification to accommodate sensory sensitivities, social energy limitations, or routine needs. This renegotiation can feel threatening to family members who value traditions or may not understand the genuine need for accommodation.

Sarah's family initially resisted her requests for modified holiday celebrations. Her need for breaks during large gatherings, preference for specific seating arrangements, and difficulty with surprise activities seemed like unreasonable demands to family members who had never seen her struggle openly. The breakthrough came when Sarah's sister attended an autism family support group and heard similar stories from other families.

Communication pattern renegotiation often represents one of the most significant relationship changes following autism diagnosis. Family members accustomed to indirect communication, emotional implications, or social subtleties may need to learn more direct, explicit communication styles. This adjustment benefits everyone but requires patience and practice from all parties.

The expectation of emotional availability may need substantial revision. Many women have provided emotional support and caretaking beyond their actual capacity, using masking to appear more available than they genuinely felt. Establishing boundaries around emotional labor and support provision can feel selfish but ultimately creates more sustainable and authentic relationships.

Social participation expectations frequently require the most dramatic adjustment. Family members may expect continued attendance at events, social gatherings, or activities that are genuinely overwhelming for autistic individuals. Negotiating selective participation, modified attendance, or alternative connection methods becomes essential for maintaining relationships without compromising wellbeing.

Setting Boundaries and Communication Needs

Establishing boundaries represents one of the most challenging aspects of relationship renegotiation, particularly for women who have learned to prioritize others' comfort over their own needs. Autism diagnosis provides both justification and framework for advocating for accommodations that support rather than challenge your neurological functioning.

Sensory boundaries often require the most immediate attention and clearest communication. Family members need specific information about sensory triggers and accommodation needs. This might involve requests for volume control during conversations, specific lighting preferences, or advance notice about environmental changes that could cause distress.

The boundary-setting process frequently reveals family dynamics that have been problematic but tolerated through masking. Some family members may resist accommodation requests, viewing them as manipulation or attention-seeking rather than genuine neurological needs. These responses often reflect family members' own discomfort with change rather than lack of caring.

Communication need boundaries encompass both style preferences and energy limitations. Many autistic women need more processing time for complex conversations, prefer written communication for important topics, or require explicit rather than implied expectations. These communication accommodations improve relationship quality while reducing misunderstandings and emotional exhaustion.

Time and energy boundaries protect against the overwhelming demands that can lead to autistic burnout. This might involve limiting phone calls to specific durations, requiring advance notice for visits, or establishing quiet time that remains uninterrupted. These boundaries can feel rejecting to family members accustomed to unlimited access.

The enforcement of boundaries requires ongoing effort and often professional support. Family therapy with autism-informed therapists can help facilitate boundary discussions while providing education about autism needs and accommodation strategies. Some family members may never fully accept boundary requirements, necessitating difficult decisions about relationship continuation.

Dealing with Denial, Rejection, or Misunderstanding

Not all family members respond to autism disclosure with acceptance and support. Denial, minimization, and outright rejection represent painful but unfortunately common responses that require emotional preparation and strategic management. Understanding these responses as reflections of others' limitations rather than evidence against your autism helps maintain self-confidence during challenging interactions.

Denial often manifests as statements like "everyone's a little autistic" or "you seem normal to me." These responses minimize your experiences while avoiding the emotional work of understanding autism's impact on your life. Family members may unconsciously resist autism acceptance because it requires acknowledging their previous misunderstanding or lack of support.

Professional diagnosis skepticism represents another common form of denial. Family members may question evaluator competence, suggest second opinions, or dismiss autism diagnosis as trendy overdiagnosis. These responses often reflect discomfort with autism labels rather than genuine concern about diagnostic accuracy.

Minimization involves acknowledging autism diagnosis while downplaying its significance or impact. Family members might say things like "it doesn't matter, you're still the same person" without understanding that accommodation and support needs have changed significantly. While well-intentioned, minimization prevents the relationship growth that authentic acceptance enables.

Rejection can take various forms, from complete dismissal of autism diagnosis to withdrawal from relationship interaction. Some family members may become uncomfortable with your autism identity, preferring to maintain previous relationship patterns despite your changed needs and understanding. This rejection often reflects their own fears and limitations rather than judgment of your worth.

Developing coping strategies for negative family responses becomes essential for emotional protection. This might involve limiting disclosure to supportive family members, reducing contact with rejecting relatives, or seeking professional support for processing family rejection. Building chosen family relationships can provide the acceptance and understanding that biological family members may be unable or unwilling to offer.

Building Supportive Relationship Dynamics

Successful relationship renegotiation following autism diagnosis creates stronger, more authentic connections based on genuine understanding rather than masked accommodation. Family members who embrace autism education and accommodation often develop deeper appreciation for your authentic self while improving their own communication and relationship skills.

Educational resources help supportive family members understand autism beyond initial disclosure conversations. Books, websites, and support groups specifically for autism families provide ongoing learning opportunities. Some family members become autism advocates, educating others and working to increase understanding and acceptance in their communities.

Accommodation implementation requires collaboration and creativity from all family members. Simple modifications like providing quiet spaces during gatherings, offering advance notice about schedule changes, or using explicit communication can dramatically improve relationship quality. These accommodations often benefit other family members as well, creating more inclusive and comfortable environments for everyone.

Regular check-ins about relationship functioning help ensure that accommodations remain effective while identifying areas needing adjustment. These conversations provide opportunities to express appreciation for supportive efforts while addressing ongoing challenges constructively. Open communication about autism needs prevents misunderstandings while strengthening family bonds.

Celebration of autism-related strengths helps family members develop positive associations with autism identity. Recognizing your attention to detail, loyalty, honesty, or special interest expertise helps balance any challenges accommodation might require. This strength-based approach improves family dynamics while building confidence in autism identity.

Professional family support can accelerate relationship improvement while providing neutral guidance for accommodation strategies. Family therapy with autism-knowledgeable providers helps navigate complex emotions while developing practical solutions for common challenges. Support groups connect families with others facing similar adjustments, reducing isolation while building community.

Moving Forward Together

Relationship renegotiation following autism diagnosis represents an opportunity for deeper authenticity and connection, though it requires effort and flexibility from all parties. Some relationships strengthen through increased understanding and accommodation, while others may need to change or end if mutual respect and support aren't possible.

The process of explaining autism, setting boundaries, and building supportive dynamics often extends over months or years as family members adjust to new understanding and accommodation needs. Patience with this process, combined with firm advocacy for your needs, creates the best foundation for successful relationship evolution.

Key Insights from Relationship Reimagination

- Autism disclosure often requires education about autism in women and explanation of specific impact on your experiences
- Relationship expectations typically need renegotiation around social participation, communication styles, and emotional availability
- Boundary setting protects your wellbeing while teaching others how to interact supportively
- Denial and rejection responses reflect others' limitations rather than evidence against your autism
- Supportive family dynamics develop through education, accommodation, and ongoing communication about autism needs

Chapter 7: Love and Partnership on the Spectrum

Romantic relationships take on unique complexity when one or both partners are autistic, particularly when autism recognition comes after relationship patterns have already been established. The discovery of autism within an existing partnership requires renegotiation of communication styles, intimacy patterns, and daily routines that may have been sources of conflict or misunderstanding. For single autistic women, dating involves strategic decisions about disclosure timing while navigating neurotypical expectations that may feel foreign or exhausting.

Dating as an Autistic Adult

The dating landscape presents particular challenges for autistic women who have spent years masking their authentic selves in social situations. Traditional dating protocols—small talk, reading social cues, managing sensory challenges in crowded restaurants—can feel overwhelming and inauthentic. Yet many autistic women desire romantic connection and companionship, requiring development of dating strategies that honor both their autism needs and relationship goals.

Online dating platforms can provide advantages for autistic women by allowing initial communication through writing rather than face-to-face interaction. Text-based communication enables more thoughtful responses without the pressure of immediate verbal replies or nonverbal interpretation. Many women report feeling more authentic and confident when they can process and respond to messages at their own pace.

Profile creation offers opportunities to subtly communicate autism-friendly preferences without explicit disclosure. Mentioning preferences for quiet restaurants, interest in deep conversations, or appreciation for direct communication can attract compatible partners while deterring those seeking more conventional dating experiences.

These preferences often appeal to other neurodivergent individuals or highly sensitive people who appreciate similar environments and communication styles.

Maria's online dating experience illustrates both the possibilities and challenges of autistic dating. She crafted her profile to emphasize her love of detailed conversations about specific topics, her preference for planned activities over spontaneous adventures, and her enjoyment of quiet environments. While this approach resulted in fewer matches, the connections she made aligned better with her authentic interests and needs.

First date planning requires consideration of sensory environments, social energy demands, and escape strategies if overwhelming situations arise. Coffee shops during off-peak hours provide controlled environments with manageable noise levels and easy exit options. Museums, bookstores, or other special interest-related venues offer conversation topics while accommodating sensory needs better than crowded bars or loud restaurants.

The energy management aspect of dating often surprises autistic women who haven't recognized their social battery limitations. What neurotypical individuals consider a pleasant evening out can feel exhausting when you're managing sensory input, monitoring social cues, and maintaining conversation for extended periods. Building recovery time into dating schedules becomes essential for sustained romantic exploration.

Disclosure Decisions and Timing

The question of when and how to disclose autism diagnosis represents one of the most complex decisions in autistic dating. Early disclosure risks rejection based on stereotypes and misconceptions, while delayed disclosure may feel deceptive if masking has hidden significant aspects of your authentic self. Most successful approaches involve gradual authenticity increase rather than dramatic revelation.

Research by Dewinter et al. (2021)[14] found that disclosure timing significantly impacts relationship outcomes, with moderate disclosure (after initial connection but before serious commitment) yielding the best results for long-term relationship satisfaction. This timing allows potential partners to connect with your authentic personality while providing education about autism before deeper emotional investment occurs.

Gradual disclosure often begins with mentioning specific autism-related preferences without using diagnostic labels. Discussing sensory sensitivities, communication preferences, or routine needs provides information about your authentic self while gauging potential partner responses. Partners who accommodate these preferences naturally often prove more compatible regardless of their autism knowledge.

Sarah's disclosure approach involved sharing specific examples rather than abstract concepts. She mentioned her need for advance notice about plan changes, her sensitivity to certain restaurant environments, and her preference for explicit communication about expectations. Her eventual partner, David, found these qualities refreshing rather than problematic, appreciating her honesty and directness.

Formal autism disclosure conversations require careful preparation and appropriate timing. Many women choose to disclose after several dates when mutual interest is established but before physical intimacy or serious commitment discussions. This timing allows for education and processing while avoiding the vulnerability that comes with deeper emotional investment.

The disclosure conversation itself benefits from focusing on specific examples rather than diagnostic labels alone. Explaining how autism affects your communication style, sensory needs, and relationship preferences provides practical information partners can use immediately. Emphasizing autism as a neurological difference rather than a disorder helps frame the conversation positively.

Educational resources can support disclosure conversations by providing partners with accurate information about autism in women.

47

Books, articles, or videos specifically addressing autism in relationships help partners understand your experiences while addressing common misconceptions about autism and compatibility.

Communication Strategies for Romantic Relationships

Autistic communication styles often differ significantly from neurotypical romantic communication expectations, particularly around emotional expression, conflict resolution, and daily interaction patterns. Successful autism-inclusive relationships require explicit discussion of communication preferences while developing strategies that work for both partners.

Direct communication preferences can initially surprise neurotypical partners accustomed to emotional implications and subtext in romantic relationships. Many autistic women prefer explicit statements about feelings, needs, and expectations rather than hints or indirect suggestions. This communication style, while initially unfamiliar to some partners, often improves relationship satisfaction by reducing misunderstandings and guesswork.

Emotional processing differences frequently require accommodation in romantic relationships. Many autistic women need additional time to identify and articulate their feelings, particularly during conflict or stressful situations. Partners may need to learn patience with processing time while developing strategies for revisiting emotional conversations when both parties feel prepared.

The concept of "emotional translations" helps bridge communication gaps between autistic and neurotypical partners. This involves explicitly discussing what specific behaviors, words, or expressions mean for each partner rather than assuming universal understanding. What appears as withdrawal to a neurotypical partner might represent overwhelm management for an autistic partner.

Jennifer's relationship with her partner Marcus required significant communication negotiation after her autism diagnosis. Marcus initially interpreted Jennifer's need for alone time as relationship

48

dissatisfaction, while Jennifer found his emotional expressiveness overwhelming and difficult to interpret. Through couples therapy with an autism-informed therapist, they developed explicit communication protocols that honored both their needs.

Conflict resolution strategies often need modification to accommodate autism-related communication patterns. Many autistic women find real-time conflict resolution overwhelming and prefer written communication or scheduled discussion times for addressing relationship issues. This approach allows for emotional regulation and thoughtful response formulation rather than reactive communication.

Regular relationship check-ins provide structure for ongoing communication about satisfaction, challenges, and accommodation needs. These scheduled conversations help prevent small issues from escalating while ensuring both partners' needs receive attention. The predictability of scheduled discussions often appeals to autistic partners while providing neurotypical partners with regular emotional connection opportunities.

Sensory Considerations in Intimacy

Physical intimacy involves complex sensory experiences that can be particularly intense for autistic individuals. Sensory sensitivities to touch, smell, sound, or visual input can significantly impact romantic and sexual experiences, requiring open communication and creative accommodation strategies. Understanding and addressing these sensory aspects often improves intimacy satisfaction for both partners.

Touch sensitivity varies dramatically among autistic individuals, with some being hypersensitive to light touch while others crave deep pressure input. Understanding your specific touch preferences and communicating them clearly to partners helps create positive intimate experiences while avoiding sensory overwhelm or discomfort.

Environmental factors significantly impact intimate experiences for many autistic women. Lighting levels, temperature, background noise, and even fabric textures can affect comfort and arousal. Creating sensory-friendly intimate environments often involves experimentation and explicit communication about preferences and sensitivities.

The unpredictability of intimate encounters can create anxiety for autistic individuals who benefit from routine and advance preparation. Some couples find that discussing intimacy plans, establishing clear consent communication, and creating predictable environmental conditions improve satisfaction while reducing anxiety for autistic partners.

Sensory breaks during intimate activities may be necessary for regulation and comfort. Understanding that these breaks reflect sensory needs rather than lack of interest helps partners accommodate autism-related requirements without taking them personally. Building acceptance of sensory regulation needs into intimate relationships creates more positive experiences for everyone involved.

Communication about sensory preferences requires ongoing attention as needs may change based on stress levels, hormonal cycles, or other factors affecting sensory processing. Regular check-ins about sensory comfort and preferences help maintain positive intimate experiences while addressing changing needs.

Building Autism-Affirming Partnerships

Successful romantic relationships involving autistic partners require active acceptance and appreciation of autism-related traits rather than mere tolerance of differences. Autism-affirming partnerships celebrate autistic strengths while providing accommodation for challenges, creating relationships where autistic partners can thrive authentically.

Partner education about autism represents a crucial component of affirming relationships. Partners who invest time in learning about autism, particularly female presentations, develop better understanding of their autistic partner's experiences and needs. This education helps distinguish between autism-related traits and relationship issues requiring different approaches.

Accommodation implementation requires creativity and collaboration from both partners. This might involve modified social schedules that honor energy limitations, environmental changes that address sensory needs, or communication adaptations that improve understanding. Successful accommodations benefit both partners by creating more harmonious living and relationship environments.

The concept of "autism mentoring" involves autistic partners educating their neurotypical partners about autism while neurotypical partners help with neurotypical world navigation. This mutual support model creates interdependence and appreciation rather than caretaking dynamics that can damage relationship equality.

Celebration of autism-related strengths helps partners develop positive associations with autism traits. Recognizing and appreciating qualities like honesty, loyalty, attention to detail, or deep knowledge in special interest areas helps balance any accommodation requirements while building confidence in autism identity.

Social navigation as a couple requires explicit planning and communication about autism needs in various situations. This might involve developing strategies for parties, family gatherings, or professional events that allow autistic partners to participate comfortably while meeting couple social obligations.

Crisis planning helps couples prepare for autism-related challenges like sensory overload, meltdowns, or burnout episodes. Having predetermined strategies for managing these situations reduces stress while ensuring appropriate support during difficult times.

Final Reflections on Love and Spectrum Living

Romantic relationships involving autism require intention, communication, and mutual respect, but can achieve remarkable depth and satisfaction when both partners commit to understanding and accommodation. The authenticity that autism diagnosis enables often strengthens relationships by eliminating the exhausting performance that masking requires.

The journey toward autism-affirming partnership involves ongoing learning, adaptation, and growth for both individuals involved. While challenges exist, many couples report that autism-informed relationship strategies improve their connection and communication beyond what they experienced in previous relationships.

Key Insights from Love and Partnership

- Online dating platforms often provide autism-friendly initial communication opportunities
- Gradual disclosure typically yields better outcomes than immediate or delayed autism revelation
- Direct communication preferences often improve relationship satisfaction despite initial adjustment requirements
- Sensory considerations significantly impact intimate experiences and require explicit discussion and accommodation
- Autism-affirming partnerships celebrate autistic traits while providing necessary accommodations for challenges

Chapter 8: Parenting and Autism

The intersection of autism diagnosis with parenting creates a unique constellation of challenges and opportunities. Late-diagnosed mothers often find themselves simultaneously learning about their own autism while potentially recognizing similar traits in their children. This dual discovery process can feel overwhelming yet profoundly validating, as patterns that seemed like family quirks suddenly make sense through an autism lens. The journey requires developing new parenting strategies while processing your own childhood experiences and unmet needs.

Autistic Parenting Strengths and Challenges

Autistic mothers bring distinctive strengths to parenting that often go unrecognized in neurotypical-centered parenting advice. The attention to detail that characterizes autism can translate into careful observation of children's needs, thorough research of parenting approaches, and consistent implementation of routines that benefit entire families. Many autistic mothers excel at creating structured, predictable environments that help children feel secure and supported.

The intense focus capability associated with autism often enhances parenting effectiveness when applied to child development and education. Rebecca, diagnosed at thirty-eight while homeschooling her two children, discovered that her natural tendency toward systematic thinking made her exceptionally effective at curriculum planning and individualized instruction. Her detailed tracking of her children's progress and careful adaptation of teaching methods reflected autism-related strengths rather than excessive parenting behaviors.

Special interests can become powerful parenting tools when they align with children's developmental needs or academic subjects. Maria's fascination with child development and educational psychology, initially dismissed as obsessive reading, proved invaluable when her daughter struggled with learning differences. Her extensive knowledge enabled early identification of issues and effective advocacy within educational systems.

The challenges of autistic parenting often relate to sensory overwhelm and executive function demands rather than lack of caring or competence. The constant noise, unpredictability, and multitasking requirements of parenting can exceed autistic mothers' processing capacity, leading to exhaustion and overwhelm that may be misinterpreted as inadequate parenting.

Social expectations around maternal intuition can create additional pressure for autistic mothers who rely more on observation and research than emotional instinct for parenting decisions. The myth that mothers naturally know what their children need can leave autistic women feeling inadequate when they require explicit information or systematic approaches to understand their children's communications.

Executive function challenges can impact daily parenting logistics without affecting the quality of emotional connection or care provision. Difficulty with meal planning, schedule management, or organizational tasks may require accommodation strategies rather than reflecting parenting deficits. Many autistic mothers benefit from external structure and support systems that free their energy for the relational aspects of parenting they value most.

Recognizing Autism in Your Children

Late autism diagnosis often occurs in the context of seeking help for children's developmental differences, creating situations where mothers recognize their own autism traits while learning about their children's needs. This simultaneous recognition process can feel overwhelming but often provides valuable insight into family patterns and effective intervention strategies.

The genetic component of autism means that autistic parents have higher likelihood of having autistic children, though autism expression varies significantly even within families. Understanding autism as a neurological difference rather than a defect helps parents approach potential child autism with acceptance rather than fear, focusing on support needs rather than cure-seeking.

Early autism signs in children may be normalized within autistic families where traits like intense interests, sensory sensitivities, or communication differences seem unremarkable. While this acceptance creates supportive environments, it can also delay recognition of support needs that could benefit children's development and social navigation.

Jennifer's recognition of autism in her five-year-old daughter Emma occurred gradually as she learned about her own autism presentation. Emma's intense focus on specific activities, her distress over clothing textures, and her precise language patterns seemed familiar rather than concerning until Jennifer understood these traits through an autism lens. This recognition led to early intervention services that supported Emma's development while validating family characteristics.

The process of evaluating children for autism often triggers parental self-recognition, particularly when detailed developmental histories reveal patterns that seemed normal within family context but reflect autism traits from clinical perspectives. Many mothers report that completing autism screening questionnaires for their children felt like describing themselves at similar ages.

Gender differences in autism presentation mean that autistic mothers may be particularly skilled at recognizing autism in daughters whose traits might be missed by professionals unfamiliar with female autism presentations. The masking and camouflaging behaviors that autistic mothers developed themselves become recognizable in their daughters' social adaptations.

Creating Autism-Friendly Family Environments

Families with autistic members benefit from environmental modifications that support sensory processing, executive function, and emotional regulation for all family members. These adaptations often improve family functioning broadly while providing essential support for autistic individuals' wellbeing and success.

Sensory environment planning becomes crucial for families with multiple autistic members who may have different or conflicting sensory needs. This might involve creating quiet spaces for regulation, managing lighting and sound levels throughout the home, or establishing sensory break areas where family members can retreat when overwhelmed.

The implementation of visual schedules, predictable routines, and clear expectations benefits both autistic parents and children by reducing anxiety and improving family functioning. These systems provide structure that supports executive function while creating predictability that helps everyone navigate daily activities more successfully.

Communication modifications often improve family dynamics when autism affects multiple family members. Using clear, direct language rather than hints or implications, providing processing time for complex discussions, and establishing explicit rules for family interactions can dramatically reduce misunderstandings and conflict.

Sarah's family transformation after autism recognition illustrates the power of autism-informed family environments. She implemented visual schedules for morning and evening routines, created sensory-friendly lighting throughout their home, and established quiet time protocols that respected everyone's need for regulation. These changes reduced daily stress while improving family harmony.

Special interest incorporation into family life can strengthen bonds while honoring autism-related passions. Families might plan vacations around special interests, create learning opportunities that build on intense interests, or use special interests as bonding activities between autistic parents and children.

The concept of "autism family culture" involves developing family values and practices that celebrate autism traits while providing necessary support. This might include appreciation for honesty and directness, acceptance of sensory needs and regulation behaviors, or validation of intense interests and detailed knowledge.

Advocating for Your Children

Autistic mothers often become fierce advocates for their children's needs, drawing on their own experiences of misunderstanding and inadequate support to ensure better outcomes for the next generation. This advocacy requires navigating educational, medical, and social systems while teaching children self-advocacy skills for independence.

Educational advocacy represents one of the most crucial areas for autistic parents, particularly given the frequent misunderstanding of autism in school settings. Understanding legal rights, effective accommodation strategies, and communication approaches that promote collaboration rather than conflict becomes essential for ensuring appropriate educational support.

The development of Individualized Education Programs (IEPs) or 504 plans requires detailed knowledge of autism presentations and effective interventions. Autistic mothers often excel at providing comprehensive information about their children's needs while advocating for specific accommodations based on their own experiences with similar challenges.

Medical advocacy involves finding healthcare providers who understand autism while ensuring that medical needs receive appropriate attention despite communication differences or sensory challenges. This might involve preparing children for medical appointments, requesting accommodations during procedures, or educating providers about autism presentations.

Maria's advocacy for her autistic son David required persistence and education across multiple systems. She researched evidence-based interventions, connected with other autism families for support and information, and developed detailed documentation of David's needs and progress. Her systematic approach, reflecting her own autism traits, proved highly effective in securing appropriate services.

Social advocacy involves teaching children to navigate neurotypical expectations while maintaining their authentic selves. This includes building self-advocacy skills, developing strategies for managing social challenges, and creating support networks that appreciate autism traits.

The balance between advocacy and independence requires careful consideration as children mature. Teaching children to advocate for themselves while providing support and guidance helps prepare them for adult independence while ensuring their needs receive recognition and accommodation.

Building Neurodivergent Family Identity

Families with multiple autistic members often develop distinctive cultures that celebrate neurodiversity while addressing shared challenges. This family identity can provide strength and resilience while creating environments where autism traits are valued rather than merely tolerated.

Autism acceptance within families involves moving beyond simple tolerance of differences to active appreciation of autism-related strengths. This might include celebrating intense interests, appreciating honest communication, or valuing the attention to detail that autistic family members provide.

The concept of "neurotype diversity" helps families understand that neurological differences contribute to family strength and resilience. Different family members may excel in various areas—one might provide emotional sensitivity, another systematic thinking, and another creative problem-solving approaches.

Tradition modification often becomes necessary in neurodivergent families to accommodate sensory sensitivities, social energy limitations, or routine needs. This might involve altered holiday celebrations, modified family gatherings, or new traditions that better serve family members' authentic needs.

Challenge navigation as a family unit involves developing strategies for managing autism-related difficulties while maintaining family cohesion and support. This includes planning for meltdowns, managing sensory overwhelm, and addressing social challenges that affect multiple family members.

Community building with other neurodivergent families provides validation, support, and practical resources for navigating shared challenges. These connections often become crucial sources of information, advocacy support, and social opportunities for both parents and children.

The development of family pride in neurodivergent identity helps children develop positive self-concept while building resilience against external judgment or misunderstanding. This pride encompasses both autism traits and the family's unique approaches to navigating the world authentically.

Wisdom for the Path Ahead

Parenting as an autistic individual while potentially raising autistic children creates complex but often deeply rewarding family dynamics. The shared understanding of autism-related experiences can strengthen family bonds while providing natural accommodation and acceptance that many autism families struggle to achieve.

The journey requires ongoing learning, adaptation, and advocacy, but often results in family environments where authenticity, acceptance, and accommodation become core values that benefit all members regardless of neurotype.

Key Insights from Autistic Parenting

- Autistic parenting strengths include attention to detail, systematic thinking, and thorough research approaches

- Recognition of autism in children often occurs simultaneously with parental self-recognition
- Autism-friendly family environments benefit all members through sensory accommodation and clear communication
- Advocacy skills become essential for ensuring children receive appropriate support across various systems
- Neurodivergent family identity can provide strength, acceptance, and positive autism-related self-concept

Chapter 9: Career Navigation

The professional world presents unique challenges for autistic women who must navigate neurotypical workplace cultures while managing sensory sensitivities, social communication differences, and executive function variations. Late autism diagnosis often reframes career struggles and successes, providing new understanding of workplace patterns while opening possibilities for more authentic professional engagement. The key lies not in hiding autism traits but in finding environments and strategies that allow your authentic strengths to flourish.

Disclosure Decisions in Professional Settings

The choice whether to disclose autism in workplace settings represents one of the most complex decisions autistic women face in their careers. Legal protections exist for disclosed disabilities, but discrimination persists despite legislation, and many women fear that autism disclosure will limit opportunities rather than provide necessary accommodations. Strategic thinking about disclosure timing, scope, and approach becomes essential for career success.

Research by Baldwin et al. (2021)[15] indicates that workplace autism disclosure outcomes vary dramatically based on organizational culture, supervisor attitudes, and the specific accommodations requested. Companies with established disability inclusion programs typically respond more positively to autism disclosure, while organizations lacking diversity awareness may react with confusion or discrimination.

The decision matrix for workplace disclosure includes multiple factors: job security, accommodation needs, relationship quality with supervisors, organizational culture, and career advancement goals. Some women choose never to disclose formally while implementing informal accommodations that improve their functioning without requiring official recognition of disability status.

Gradual disclosure strategies often prove more successful than immediate revelation. This might involve initially requesting accommodations without mentioning autism, gauging supervisor and colleague responses to diversity discussions, or sharing autism information with trusted colleagues before formal disclosure to management.

Jennifer's disclosure experience illustrates both potential benefits and challenges of workplace autism revelation. Working as a software developer, she initially struggled with open office noise levels and frequent interruptions that disrupted her concentration. After her autism diagnosis, she chose to disclose to her immediate supervisor, requesting noise-canceling headphones and blocks of uninterrupted time for complex coding tasks. Her supervisor, impressed by Jennifer's work quality, readily approved these accommodations, leading to significant productivity improvements.

However, disclosure doesn't always yield positive results. Maria encountered skepticism from her supervisor who questioned the validity of her autism diagnosis, suggesting that she seemed "too competent" to need accommodations. This response required additional education and advocacy, ultimately leading Maria to seek support from her company's human resources department.

Selective disclosure involves sharing autism information with specific individuals while maintaining privacy with others. Many women choose to disclose to direct supervisors for accommodation purposes while keeping the information private from colleagues who might not need to know. This approach provides necessary support while limiting potential negative responses.

Requesting Accommodations Effectively

Effective accommodation requests require clear communication about specific needs while connecting those needs to job performance improvements rather than personal preferences. Understanding your autism-related challenges and their workplace impact enables targeted accommodation strategies that benefit both employee wellbeing and organizational productivity.

The Americans with Disabilities Act (ADA) requires employers to provide reasonable accommodations that enable disabled employees to perform essential job functions. For autistic employees, common accommodations include environmental modifications, communication adaptations, schedule flexibility, and task structure adjustments.

Environmental accommodations address sensory challenges that can significantly impact autistic employees' functioning. These might include lighting modifications, noise reduction strategies, workspace location changes, or permission to use sensory tools like noise-canceling headphones or fidget devices during work hours.

Communication accommodations help bridge differences between autistic communication styles and neurotypical workplace expectations. This might involve receiving instructions in writing rather than verbally, having explicit expectations rather than implied requirements, or being provided with agenda items before meetings to allow processing time.

Schedule accommodations address executive function challenges and sensory sensitivity variations that affect optimal working times. Some autistic employees function better during specific hours, need longer breaks for regulation, or require advance notice about schedule changes that might disrupt their routines.

The accommodation request process benefits from thorough preparation and professional presentation. Creating detailed documentation of specific needs, their workplace impact, and proposed solutions demonstrates professionalism while providing clear information for supervisor decision-making.

Sarah's accommodation success resulted from systematic presentation of her needs and proposed solutions. She documented how fluorescent lighting caused headaches that affected her concentration, researched lighting alternatives available through the company's facilities department, and proposed specific modifications that would improve her productivity. Her supervisor appreciated the thorough analysis and readily approved the lighting changes.

Playing to Autistic Strengths in Career Choices

Many autistic women discover that career satisfaction correlates strongly with environments that utilize their autism-related strengths while minimizing challenges. Understanding these patterns can guide career choices, job searches, and professional development strategies that align with authentic capabilities and interests.

Systematic thinking and attention to detail represent significant autistic strengths that align well with careers in fields like engineering, computer science, research, accounting, and quality control. These professions often value precision, thoroughness, and analytical thinking that come naturally to many autistic individuals.

Pattern recognition abilities can translate into success in careers involving data analysis, research, troubleshooting, or detective work. Many autistic women excel at identifying inconsistencies, analyzing complex information, and developing systematic approaches to problem-solving.

Intense interests often become career assets when they align with professional opportunities. Women whose special interests involve specific academic subjects, technical skills, or creative pursuits may find career satisfaction in fields that utilize these passionate knowledge areas.

Honest communication and ethical thinking represent valuable traits in professions requiring integrity and transparent communication. Many autistic women find satisfaction in careers like social work, advocacy, teaching, or healthcare where their natural honesty and commitment to fairness become professional strengths.

The preference for routine and predictability can be advantageous in careers that involve structured processes, established procedures, or systematic approaches. Administrative roles, technical positions, or specialized professional services often provide the predictability that helps autistic employees thrive.

Rebecca's career transformation after autism diagnosis illustrates the power of aligning work with authentic strengths. Previously struggling in a customer service role that required constant social interaction and emotional labor, she transitioned to a data analysis position that utilized her pattern recognition abilities and preference for independent work. Her productivity and job satisfaction improved dramatically in the environment that matched her autism-related capabilities.

Managing Workplace Social Dynamics

Workplace social expectations can present significant challenges for autistic women who may struggle with office politics, small talk, team dynamics, and unwritten social rules that govern professional interactions. Developing strategies for managing these social aspects becomes crucial for career advancement while maintaining authentic self-expression.

Understanding workplace culture requires careful observation and sometimes explicit instruction about unwritten rules that neurotypical employees absorb intuitively. This might involve learning about appropriate communication styles, meeting etiquette, professional relationship boundaries, or informal social expectations.

Small talk and casual conversation represent particular challenges for many autistic women who prefer meaningful, purpose-driven communication. Developing scripts for common social interactions, learning to redirect conversations toward topics of genuine interest, or finding colleagues who share deeper conversation preferences can help navigate these requirements.

Team collaboration often requires adaptation strategies that honor autism-related working styles while meeting group expectations. This might involve requesting written meeting summaries, contributing specialized expertise rather than general input, or finding ways to participate authentically in group problem-solving processes.

Networking events and professional social gatherings can feel overwhelming due to sensory challenges and social demands. Strategies might include attending smaller professional groups, preparing conversation topics in advance, limiting event duration, or finding one-on-one networking opportunities that feel more manageable.

Office politics navigation requires understanding implicit power dynamics and relationship patterns that may not be obvious to autistic individuals who prefer direct communication. Finding trusted colleagues who can provide insight into organizational dynamics often proves invaluable for career advancement.

The concept of "professional masking" involves adapting autism traits for workplace success while maintaining authentic core identity. This might mean learning to express enthusiasm in neurotypically expected ways while pursuing genuine interests, or developing professional versions of natural communication styles.

Building Professional Support Networks

Creating supportive professional relationships becomes essential for career success, particularly for autistic women who may need additional guidance navigating neurotypical workplace expectations. These networks provide both practical career support and social connection that enhances professional satisfaction.

Mentorship relationships can provide invaluable guidance for career development while offering opportunities to learn from others' experiences navigating professional challenges. Autism-informed mentors understand neurodivergent perspectives, while neurotypical mentors can provide insight into mainstream professional expectations.

Professional autism networks offer specific support for autistic individuals navigating career challenges. Organizations like the Autistic Self Advocacy Network (ASAN) or local autism professional groups provide resources, networking opportunities, and advocacy support for workplace issues.

Employee resource groups (ERGs) focused on disability inclusion or neurodiversity can provide workplace support while advocating for systemic improvements that benefit all disabled employees. These groups often offer professional development opportunities specifically designed for neurodivergent individuals.

Allies within organizations become crucial advocates for autism acceptance and accommodation. These colleagues, who may or may not be disabled themselves, provide support during challenging situations while helping educate others about autism and workplace inclusion.

Professional development opportunities specifically designed for autistic individuals help build career skills while providing community connection with others facing similar challenges. These might include autism-focused professional conferences, skill-building workshops, or career coaching services.

The development of "career insurance" through skill building, network expansion, and financial planning provides security for autistic women who may face employment challenges due to discrimination or accommodation difficulties. This preparation enables career resilience while building confidence for professional advocacy.

Professional Growth and Development

Career advancement for autistic women often requires strategic planning that accounts for autism-related strengths and challenges while building skills needed for professional success. This growth process may look different from neurotypical career development but can achieve remarkable success when aligned with authentic capabilities.

Skill development priorities should focus on areas that enhance autistic strengths while building competencies needed for career goals. This might involve technical skill advancement that utilizes systematic thinking, communication training that adapts natural honesty for professional contexts, or leadership development that builds on autism-related integrity and attention to detail.

Performance review preparation helps ensure that autism-related contributions receive recognition while addressing any challenges constructively. Documenting specific achievements, preparing examples of problem-solving approaches, and communicating value-added contributions helps supervisors understand autistic employees' unique professional strengths.

Leadership opportunities may require adaptation strategies that honor autism-related leadership styles while meeting organizational expectations. Many autistic women lead effectively through expertise, systematic thinking, and ethical decision-making rather than traditional charismatic approaches.

Career transition planning becomes particularly important for autistic women who may need to change positions due to accommodation needs, organizational culture shifts, or evolving career interests. Building transferable skills, maintaining professional networks, and understanding legal rights helps ensure successful transitions.

Entrepreneurship represents an attractive option for many autistic women who struggle with traditional workplace environments. Starting businesses based on special interests, utilizing autism-related strengths, or creating autism-friendly work environments enables professional success while maintaining authentic self-expression.

Professional Wisdom

Career success as an autistic woman requires balancing authentic self-expression with professional effectiveness, often involving creative solutions and strategic thinking about when and how to advocate for needs. The goal isn't to eliminate autism traits but to find professional environments and strategies that allow those traits to contribute meaningfully to career satisfaction and advancement.

Understanding your autism-related patterns, strengths, and challenges enables strategic career decisions that align with your authentic capabilities while building toward meaningful professional goals.

Key Insights from Career Navigation

- Disclosure decisions require strategic thinking about timing, scope, and organizational culture
- Effective accommodation requests connect specific needs to job performance improvements
- Career satisfaction often increases when work environments utilize autism-related strengths
- Workplace social dynamics require conscious strategy development and supportive relationships
- Professional success comes through aligning authentic capabilities with meaningful career opportunities

Chapter 10: Self-Advocacy

The journey from autism diagnosis to effective self-advocacy represents one of the most transformative aspects of late recognition. After years of accommodating others' expectations while suppressing your own needs, learning to articulate requirements and advocate for accommodations requires developing entirely new skills. Self-advocacy extends beyond requesting specific modifications to encompass confident communication about your needs, rights, and value as an autistic individual in various life contexts.

Understanding Your Rights and Accommodations

Legal protections for disabled individuals exist across multiple domains, but understanding these rights and effectively advocating for their implementation requires knowledge, preparation, and persistence. The Americans with Disabilities Act (ADA), Section 504 of the Rehabilitation Act, and various state and local laws provide frameworks for accommodation and non-discrimination, though enforcement often depends on individual advocacy efforts.

Workplace rights under the ADA include reasonable accommodations that enable disabled employees to perform essential job functions without creating undue burden for employers. For autistic individuals, these accommodations might address sensory environments, communication preferences, schedule modifications, or task structure adaptations that improve functioning and productivity.

Educational rights encompass both K-12 protections under the Individuals with Disabilities Education Act (IDEA) and higher education accommodations under Section 504 and the ADA. Adult learners returning to education after autism diagnosis can access accommodations like extended test time, alternative testing environments, note-taking assistance, or course modification that address autism-related learning differences.

Housing rights include reasonable modifications to policies, procedures, or physical structures that enable disabled individuals to access and enjoy housing opportunities. This might involve modifications to noise restrictions, pet policies for emotional support animals, or physical modifications that address sensory sensitivities.

Public accommodation rights ensure access to businesses, transportation, and public services. Understanding these rights helps autistic individuals advocate for sensory accommodations, communication assistance, or service modifications that enable full participation in community activities.

Healthcare rights include communication accommodations, sensory modifications, and appointment scheduling adjustments that address autism-related needs. Many autistic individuals benefit from written instructions, longer appointment times, or environmental modifications that reduce sensory overwhelm during medical visits.

The key to effective rights utilization lies in understanding that accommodations should address specific functional limitations rather than general diagnostic categories. Focusing on how autism affects your ability to perform specific activities enables targeted accommodation requests that address genuine needs while demonstrating reasonable necessity.

Effective Self-Advocacy Communication

Successful self-advocacy requires developing communication skills that convey your needs clearly while building collaborative relationships with accommodation providers. This involves balancing assertiveness with diplomacy, providing necessary information while maintaining appropriate boundaries, and demonstrating problem-solving collaboration rather than demanding special treatment.

The structure of effective accommodation requests includes several key components: clear description of your disability and its functional impact, specific accommodation needs, connection between accommodations and improved performance, and willingness to explore alternative solutions that meet mutual needs.

Documentation strengthens accommodation requests by providing professional validation of your needs and their legitimacy. This might include diagnostic reports, letter from healthcare providers, or functional assessments that demonstrate specific impacts of autism on relevant activities.

Sarah's workplace accommodation request illustrates effective advocacy communication. Rather than simply stating "I have autism and need accommodations," she explained: "I have autism spectrum disorder, which affects my sensory processing and concentration. The open office environment with fluorescent lighting and constant noise makes it difficult for me to focus on detailed analytical work. I'm requesting permission to use noise-canceling headphones and work from a quieter location during tasks requiring sustained concentration. These accommodations would improve my productivity and accuracy on data analysis projects."

The tone of accommodation requests significantly impacts their reception. Approaching requests as collaborative problem-solving rather than demands for special treatment encourages positive responses while building supportive relationships with supervisors, educators, or service providers.

Follow-up communication helps ensure successful accommodation implementation while addressing any challenges that arise during the process. Regular check-ins about accommodation effectiveness demonstrate your commitment to making arrangements work while providing opportunities to refine approaches based on experience.

Written communication often proves more effective than verbal requests for many autistic individuals and accommodation providers. Email requests provide documentation of the accommodation process while allowing time for thoughtful composition and response that may improve communication quality.

Template Scripts for Common Situations

Developing prepared language for common accommodation scenarios builds confidence while ensuring clear communication about your needs. These scripts provide starting points that can be adapted for specific situations while maintaining consistent advocacy messaging.

Workplace accommodation requests might follow this template: "I have autism spectrum disorder, which affects [specific functional areas]. This impacts my ability to [specific job functions] in the current environment. I'm requesting [specific accommodations] to address these challenges. These modifications would help me [specific performance improvements] while [addressing any employer concerns]. I'm happy to discuss alternative approaches that meet both my needs and the organization's requirements."

Educational accommodation requests often require more detailed functional impact descriptions: "My autism diagnosis affects [learning functions] in classroom environments. Specifically, [detailed examples of challenges]. I'm requesting accommodations including [specific modifications] to address these barriers. These accommodations would enable me to demonstrate my knowledge and abilities more effectively while participating fully in the academic program."

Healthcare accommodation scripts focus on communication and environmental needs: "I have autism spectrum disorder, which affects my communication and sensory processing. To help ensure effective healthcare delivery, I would benefit from [specific accommodations] during appointments. These modifications help me communicate more clearly about my health concerns while managing sensory sensitivities that might interfere with examination or treatment."

Social service accommodation requests emphasize functional barriers and specific solutions: "My autism affects [relevant functional areas], creating barriers to accessing [specific services]. I'm requesting reasonable modifications including [specific accommodations] to ensure equal access to services. These accommodations address my disability-related needs while enabling full participation in available programs."

Emergency situation scripts help ensure accommodation needs are understood during crisis situations: "I have autism spectrum disorder, which affects my communication and sensory processing. During this situation, I need [specific accommodations] to participate effectively. These modifications help me understand information and communicate my needs clearly despite the stress of the current situation."

Building Confidence in Asking for Needs

Many autistic women struggle with self-advocacy due to years of learning to minimize their needs and prioritize others' comfort. Building confidence for advocacy requires both skill development and mindset shifts that validate your right to accommodation while developing tools for effective need communication.

Understanding accommodation as civil rights rather than special favors provides a crucial foundation for confident advocacy. The ADA and related legislation establish accommodation as legal requirements, not optional kindness from service providers. This perspective helps frame requests as rights enforcement rather than personal requests for special treatment.

Practice opportunities help build advocacy confidence through low-stakes scenarios that develop communication skills. Role-playing accommodation requests with trusted friends, practicing scripts in low-pressure situations, or starting with minor accommodation needs can build experience and confidence for more significant advocacy situations.

Success documentation helps build confidence by tracking positive accommodation outcomes and effective advocacy strategies. Keeping records of successful requests, helpful responses from accommodation providers, and effective communication approaches provides evidence of advocacy capability while building a resource library for future situations.

Support network development provides encouragement and guidance during challenging advocacy situations. Connecting with other autistic individuals who have navigation accommodation processes, finding allies who understand autism and support your advocacy efforts, or working with disability rights organizations can provide essential support during difficult advocacy situations.

Professional advocacy support becomes valuable for complex or contested accommodation situations. Disability rights attorneys, advocacy organizations, or professional advocates can provide expertise and support when individual advocacy efforts face resistance or require legal intervention.

The mindset shift from accommodation as burden to accommodation as mutual benefit helps build confidence while improving advocacy outcomes. Framing accommodations as improvements that benefit both disabled individuals and service providers—better employee productivity, improved customer satisfaction, enhanced educational outcomes—creates collaborative rather than adversarial advocacy relationships.

Creating Support Documentation

Comprehensive support documentation strengthens accommodation requests while providing professional validation of autism-related needs. This documentation serves multiple purposes: educating accommodation providers about autism and its functional impacts, demonstrating legitimacy of accommodation requests, and providing legal protection if discrimination occurs.

Diagnostic documentation from qualified professionals provides the foundation for accommodation requests. This should include specific diagnostic information, functional impact descriptions, and recommended accommodations based on professional assessment of your needs and challenges.

Functional impact assessments describe how autism affects your ability to perform specific activities relevant to the accommodation request context. Rather than general autism descriptions, these assessments focus on particular functional limitations that create barriers in specific environments or situations.

Professional recommendation letters from healthcare providers, therapists, or other qualified professionals add credibility to accommodation requests while providing expert perspective on necessary modifications. These letters should connect autism diagnosis to specific functional impacts while recommending particular accommodations based on professional expertise.

Previous accommodation documentation demonstrates successful accommodation use while providing evidence of ongoing needs. Records from educational institutions, previous employers, or other service providers help establish accommodation history and effectiveness.

Jennifer's documentation package for graduate school accommodations included her diagnostic report from a licensed psychologist, a letter from her therapist describing autism's impact on her learning and social functioning, documentation of successful undergraduate accommodations, and a detailed personal statement connecting her autism-related challenges to specific accommodation needs in graduate-level coursework.

Legal documentation becomes necessary if accommodation requests are denied or if discrimination occurs. Understanding how to file complaints with relevant agencies, document discrimination instances, and seek legal support helps protect your rights while encouraging compliance with accommodation requirements.

Regular documentation updates ensure that support materials remain current and relevant to changing needs or circumstances. Autism-related challenges may change over time, requiring updated documentation that reflects current functioning and accommodation requirements.

Navigating Accommodation Resistance

Despite legal protections, accommodation requests sometimes encounter resistance from employers, educators, service providers, or family members who may not understand autism or accommodation requirements. Developing strategies for addressing this resistance becomes essential for successful advocacy while maintaining relationships and achieving necessary support.

Education about autism and accommodation requirements often addresses resistance based on misunderstanding or lack of information. Providing accurate autism information, explaining specific functional impacts, and connecting accommodations to improved outcomes can transform resistant attitudes into supportive collaboration.

Professional consultation helps address resistance from accommodation providers who question the legitimacy or necessity of requested modifications. Having healthcare providers, disability rights experts, or autism specialists available for consultation can provide authoritative perspective that supports accommodation implementation.

Legal advocacy becomes necessary when accommodation resistance persists despite education and professional consultation. Understanding complaint processes, documentation requirements, and legal timelines helps protect your rights while encouraging compliance with accommodation requirements.

Alternative approach development helps address resistance while still meeting accommodation needs. If specific accommodation requests encounter resistance, exploring alternative modifications that address the same functional needs may provide solutions that work for all parties involved.

Escalation strategies provide options when initial accommodation requests are denied or inadequately addressed. This might involve requesting supervisory review, filing formal complaints, seeking mediation services, or pursuing legal action when necessary to enforce accommodation rights.

Maria's experience with workplace accommodation resistance illustrates effective advocacy persistence. When her initial request for noise-reducing accommodations was denied by her immediate supervisor, she provided additional autism education materials, requested a meeting with human resources, and ultimately received support from the company's disability coordinator who helped implement appropriate accommodations.

The emotional impact of accommodation resistance requires support and self-care strategies that maintain advocacy motivation while protecting mental health. Connecting with other autistic individuals who have faced similar challenges, working with therapists who understand autism and advocacy stress, or participating in disability rights communities can provide essential support during difficult advocacy situations.

Wisdom for Advocacy Success

Self-advocacy represents both a skill set and a mindset that develops over time through practice, education, and community support. The goal isn't perfect advocacy from the beginning but gradual development of confidence and competence in communicating your needs while building supportive relationships that honor your autism-related requirements.

Effective advocacy balances assertiveness with collaboration, rights enforcement with relationship building, and individual needs with community understanding. This balance enables sustainable advocacy that achieves accommodation goals while maintaining positive relationships with accommodation providers.

Key Insights from Self-Advocacy

- Understanding legal rights provides the foundation for confident accommodation requests
- Effective advocacy communication balances assertiveness with collaboration and education

- Template scripts build confidence while ensuring clear communication about specific needs
- Comprehensive documentation strengthens accommodation requests and provides legal protection
- Accommodation resistance requires persistent education, professional support, and sometimes legal advocacy

Chapter 11: Building Your Autism Community

The discovery of autism identity often coincides with a profound need for community—connection with others who share similar experiences, challenges, and perspectives. For women who have spent years feeling different and isolated, finding autism community can feel like coming home to a place you never knew existed. Building meaningful connections within autism communities requires navigation of diverse perspectives, online and offline spaces, and the complex dynamics that exist within any community seeking recognition and acceptance.

Finding Online and Local Autism Communities

The internet has revolutionized autism community access, providing spaces where geographic isolation, social anxiety, and communication differences need not prevent meaningful connection. Online autism communities offer 24/7 availability, diverse perspectives, and reduced social pressure that can make initial community engagement more accessible for many autistic women.

Facebook groups dedicated to autism in women have become particularly valuable resources, offering closed or private spaces where members can share experiences without judgment from the broader public. Groups like "Women with Asperger's/Autism Spectrum" or "Actually Autistic" provide platforms for discussing everything from sensory challenges to workplace discrimination, creating virtual support networks that often extend into real-life friendships.

Reddit communities such as r/aspergirls and r/AutismInWomen offer anonymous forums where women can seek advice, share experiences, and find validation for challenges that neurotypical friends might not understand. The anonymity aspect allows for honest discussion of sensitive topics while the voting system helps surface particularly helpful or resonant content.

Twitter has developed a robust "Actually Autistic" community where autistic individuals share daily experiences, advocate for better understanding, and challenge misconceptions about autism. The platform's brief format suits many autistic communication styles while the hashtag system enables connection around specific topics or interests.

Discord servers provide real-time chat opportunities that can feel more immediate than forum-based interactions while still maintaining some social distance. Many servers organize voice chats for those comfortable with verbal communication while maintaining text-based options for members who prefer written interaction.

Local autism communities vary significantly in availability and quality depending on geographic location. Urban areas typically offer more resources including support groups, social meetups, and advocacy organizations, while rural areas may require more creative approaches to finding community connection.

Sarah's community journey illustrates the progression many women experience from online discovery to local engagement. Initially finding validation through Facebook groups and Reddit discussions, she gradually built confidence to attend local Autism Society meetings, eventually becoming involved in advocacy efforts and mentoring other newly diagnosed women.

The Autistic Self Advocacy Network (ASAN) provides both online resources and local chapter opportunities for those interested in advocacy and policy work. Their emphasis on "nothing about us without us" resonates with many autistic individuals seeking authentic representation rather than parent-centered autism organizations.

Navigating Different Autism Perspectives

Autism communities encompass tremendous diversity in perspectives, experiences, and opinions about autism identity, treatment approaches, and advocacy priorities. Navigating these differences requires understanding that autism experiences vary widely while developing skills for engaging respectfully with viewpoints that may differ from your own.

The neurodiversity movement emphasizes autism as a natural neurological variation rather than a disorder requiring cure. This perspective celebrates autism traits while advocating for accommodation and acceptance rather than normalization. Many late-diagnosed women find this framework liberating after years of believing they were fundamentally flawed.

Medical model perspectives focus on autism as a developmental disability requiring intervention and support. While less popular in autistic self-advocacy communities, this viewpoint influences much professional practice and remains relevant for accessing services and accommodations.

The identity-first versus person-first language debate reflects deeper philosophical differences about autism identity. Many autistic self-advocates prefer "autistic person" to "person with autism," viewing autism as integral to identity rather than an add-on condition. Understanding these preferences helps navigate community norms respectfully.

Functioning labels represent another area of community disagreement. Terms like "high-functioning" and "low-functioning" are increasingly rejected by many autistic advocates who argue these labels obscure the complexity of autism experiences while reinforcing harmful hierarchies.

Support needs language offers more nuanced ways to discuss autism diversity, focusing on specific support requirements rather than overall functioning levels. This approach recognizes that individuals may need significant support in some areas while functioning independently in others.

Controversy exists around certain organizations, treatments, and advocacy approaches within autism communities. Understanding these divisions helps new community members navigate conversations while developing their own informed perspectives.

Jennifer found community navigation challenging initially, feeling overwhelmed by passionate debates about topics she was still learning about. She eventually learned to listen more than speak initially, gradually developing her own perspectives through education and experience rather than immediately taking sides in community controversies.

Building Meaningful Friendships

Developing genuine friendships within autism communities requires moving beyond shared diagnosis to discover compatible personalities, interests, and values. While autism provides initial connection points, sustainable friendships develop through the same qualities that strengthen any relationship: mutual respect, shared interests, and emotional compatibility.

The intensity that characterizes many autistic individuals can create profound friendships that develop quickly and deeply. Shared experiences of masking, sensory challenges, and social misunderstanding provide immediate bonds that can accelerate friendship development beyond typical neurotypical timelines.

Common interests often serve as friendship foundations, particularly when these interests align with autism-related special interests. Finding others who share your passion for specific topics, creative pursuits, or analytical activities can create friendships based on genuine enthusiasm and mutual appreciation.

Communication style compatibility becomes crucial for sustainable autism friendships. Some autistic individuals prefer direct, factual communication while others enjoy emotional expression and support. Finding friends whose communication preferences align with your own reduces misunderstandings while improving relationship satisfaction.

Sensory and social needs alignment can strengthen autism friendships by enabling mutually comfortable social activities. Friends who share similar noise sensitivities might enjoy quiet coffee shops together, while those with compatible energy levels can engage in appropriate activity types without overwhelming each other.

The concept of "parallel friendship" works well for many autistic individuals who enjoy companionship without constant interaction. These friendships might involve working on individual projects in shared spaces, participating in structured activities together, or simply appreciating each other's company without pressure for constant conversation.

Rachel's friendship with another autistic woman, Lisa, developed through their shared love of historical research and compatible communication styles. They met at a local history museum event, discovered mutual interests in genealogy and historical architecture, and gradually developed a friendship based on shared projects and comfortable, low-pressure social interaction.

Geographic challenges often affect autism friendships, as quality matches may not exist locally. Many autistic individuals maintain long-distance friendships through online communication, occasional visits, or virtual shared activities that transcend physical location limitations.

Contributing to Autism Acceptance

Moving from community membership to active contribution represents natural progression for many autistic women who have found support and validation through autism communities. Contributing to autism acceptance involves sharing your experiences, supporting other community members, and advocating for broader understanding and accommodation.

Storytelling represents one of the most powerful tools for autism acceptance, particularly when it challenges stereotypes or provides representation for underrepresented groups. Sharing your late diagnosis experience, workplace challenges, or family relationships can help others feel less alone while educating neurotypical audiences about autism realities.

Mentoring newly diagnosed women provides crucial support while helping build community knowledge and resilience. Many women benefit from guidance navigating initial post-diagnosis challenges, accommodation strategies, or community integration from others who have traveled similar paths.

Educational advocacy involves sharing accurate autism information with neurotypical communities, challenging misconceptions, and promoting acceptance-based approaches rather than cure-focused perspectives. This might include presentations to professional groups, writing articles or blog posts, or participating in autism awareness events.

Policy advocacy focuses on systemic changes that improve life conditions for autistic individuals through legislation, organizational policies, or community practices. This might involve supporting disability rights legislation, advocating for workplace inclusion policies, or promoting autism-informed practices in healthcare or education.

Research participation helps advance autism understanding while ensuring that autistic perspectives influence academic and clinical knowledge development. Participating in studies, providing feedback on research questions, or collaborating with researchers helps center autistic voices in autism research.

Maria became involved in autism acceptance through writing about her late diagnosis experience on social media. Her posts about workplace challenges and accommodation strategies resonated with other autistic women, eventually leading to speaking opportunities at professional conferences and consultation with organizations developing autism inclusion programs.

Creative expression provides another avenue for autism acceptance contribution. Art, writing, music, or other creative works that authentically represent autism experiences help expand public understanding while validating autistic perspectives and experiences.

Creating Your Support Network

Building a comprehensive support network requires intentional cultivation of relationships that provide different types of support: emotional validation, practical advice, social connection, advocacy assistance, and crisis intervention. This network typically includes both autism community members and allies from broader communities.

Professional support providers who understand autism can become crucial network members. This might include autism-informed therapists, healthcare providers familiar with autism presentations, or legal advocates who understand disability rights. These professionals provide expertise while validating autism-related experiences and needs.

Family members and friends who embrace autism acceptance become invaluable allies who can provide support across various life domains. These relationships often require education and patience but can develop into profound sources of understanding and accommodation.

Workplace allies help navigate professional challenges while advocating for inclusion and understanding in employment settings. These might include supportive supervisors, human resources professionals, or colleagues who understand and appreciate autism-related contributions.

Online support networks provide accessible assistance regardless of geographic location or time constraints. These connections often prove particularly valuable during crisis situations when immediate local support might not be available.

Crisis support planning involves identifying specific individuals and resources available during particularly challenging periods. This might include therapists with crisis training, emergency contacts who understand autism, or specific online communities that provide immediate support.

The diversity of support network needs reflects the complexity of autism experiences and life circumstances. Different situations require different types of support, making broad network development more resilient than dependence on single support sources.

Sarah's support network evolution illustrates the gradual development process many women experience. Beginning with online validation and information-seeking, she gradually built relationships with local autism community members, developed professional support relationships with autism-informed providers, and educated family members who became strong allies in her autism journey.

Reflections on Community Connection

Building autism community involves both receiving and providing support while contributing to broader acceptance and understanding. The process requires patience, discernment, and often considerable emotional investment, but typically yields profound benefits in terms of validation, practical support, and sense of belonging.

Community engagement strategies should align with your personal energy levels, interests, and life circumstances while remaining flexible enough to evolve as your needs and capacity change over time.

Key Insights from Building Autism Community

- Online communities provide accessible initial connection points with diverse support options
- Autism communities encompass various perspectives that require respectful navigation
- Meaningful friendships develop through shared interests and compatible communication styles beyond autism diagnosis
- Contributing to autism acceptance provides purpose while advancing community goals
- Comprehensive support networks include autism community members, professional providers, and allies from broader communities

Chapter 12: Thriving, Not Just Surviving

The path from autism diagnosis to authentic thriving extends far beyond initial recognition and accommodation. True flourishing involves integrating autism identity into a life aligned with your genuine values, interests, and capabilities while contributing meaningfully to your communities. This journey requires ongoing self-discovery, continuous advocacy, and the courage to pursue dreams that honor your authentic self rather than neurotypical expectations.

Celebrating Autistic Identity and Strengths

The transition from viewing autism as a problem to be solved to recognizing it as a fundamental aspect of your identity represents one of the most profound shifts in the post-diagnosis journey. This celebration doesn't ignore challenges or minimize the need for support, but rather acknowledges that autism brings distinctive strengths and perspectives that enrich both your life and the communities you engage with.

Pattern recognition abilities that characterize many autistic minds often translate into professional advantages in fields requiring analytical thinking, problem-solving, or systematic approaches. These cognitive strengths, when properly supported and developed, can lead to remarkable achievements in science, technology, arts, and numerous other domains.

Attention to detail represents another significant autistic strength that benefits both individual pursuits and collaborative efforts. The ability to notice discrepancies, maintain quality standards, and thoroughly complete complex tasks often proves invaluable in professional and personal contexts.

Intense interests, rather than being viewed as obsessions requiring management, can become sources of expertise, career direction, and personal fulfillment. Many autistic individuals develop world-class knowledge in their areas of interest, contributing valuable insights and innovations to their fields.

Honest communication styles, while sometimes challenging in neurotypical social contexts, provide authenticity and directness that many people appreciate once they understand and adjust to these communication patterns. This honesty often builds trust and meaningful relationships with those who value genuine interaction.

Systematic thinking approaches enable effective problem-solving and project management when properly channeled and supported. The preference for logical, step-by-step approaches often leads to successful outcomes in complex situations where others might feel overwhelmed.

Jennifer's journey illustrates this strength celebration process. Initially viewing her need for routine and detailed planning as limitations, she gradually recognized these traits as assets in her career as a project manager. Her systematic approach and attention to detail became valued team contributions, leading to professional advancement and increased confidence in her autism-related capabilities.

The sensory sensitivity that often challenges autistic individuals can also provide enhanced awareness and appreciation for environmental details that others miss. This heightened sensory awareness can contribute to artistic expression, environmental design, or quality assessment capabilities.

Justice-seeking and ethical thinking represent common autistic traits that benefit communities and organizations. Many autistic individuals possess strong moral compasses and commitment to fairness that translate into valuable advocacy, policy development, or ethical guidance capabilities.

Continuing Personal Growth and Discovery

Autism diagnosis marks the beginning rather than the end of self-discovery. The process of unmasking, developing authentic self-expression, and exploring previously suppressed interests often reveals capabilities and passions that remained hidden during years of accommodation and camouflaging.

Educational pursuits often take on new meaning after autism diagnosis as individuals reconnect with learning approaches that align with their authentic processing styles. Many women return to school to study autism, pursue postponed interests, or develop expertise in areas that engage their passion and systematic thinking abilities.

Creative expression frequently flourishes post-diagnosis as individuals give themselves permission to explore artistic, literary, or innovative pursuits without concern for neurotypical expectations. This creative freedom often produces distinctive work that reflects autism-related perspectives and experiences.

Relationship skills continue developing as individuals learn to communicate authentically while building connections based on genuine compatibility rather than masking-based accommodations. This often leads to more satisfying friendships and romantic relationships built on mutual understanding and acceptance.

Career evolution represents another area of ongoing growth as individuals align their professional lives with autism-related strengths while advocating for necessary accommodations. Many women make significant career changes post-diagnosis, pursuing work that better matches their authentic capabilities and interests.

Self-advocacy skills strengthen through practice and community connection, enabling more effective navigation of various life domains while building confidence for addressing challenges and pursuing opportunities.

Maria's post-diagnosis growth exemplifies this ongoing development. Initially focused on managing challenges and securing accommodations, she gradually expanded her horizons to include graduate study in her special interest area, advocacy work with autism organizations, and creative writing that reflected her autism experiences. Each area of growth built upon others, creating an integrated life that honored her autism identity while pursuing meaningful goals.

The development of emotional regulation skills often improves significantly after diagnosis as individuals understand their sensory and social needs while implementing appropriate accommodation strategies. This emotional stability provides a foundation for pursuing goals and relationships with increased confidence.

Contributing to Autism Awareness and Acceptance

Moving from personal accommodation to community contribution represents a natural progression for many autistic individuals who have found support and understanding through autism communities. Contributing to broader awareness and acceptance helps create better conditions for current and future autistic individuals while providing meaning and purpose beyond personal needs.

Educational outreach involves sharing accurate autism information with neurotypical communities while challenging stereotypes and misconceptions that perpetuate discrimination. This might include presentations to professional groups, participation in autism awareness events, or informal education within existing social and professional networks.

Representation in media and literature helps expand public understanding of autism diversity while providing role models for other autistic individuals. Writing about autism experiences, participating in documentary projects, or creating artistic works that authentically portray autism perspectives contributes to more accurate and respectful representation.

Mentoring newly diagnosed individuals provides crucial support while helping build community resilience and knowledge. Many autistic women find deep satisfaction in supporting others through challenges they have navigated themselves, creating cycles of support that strengthen autism communities.

Policy advocacy focuses on systemic changes that improve access, accommodation, and acceptance for autistic individuals across various life domains. This might involve supporting disability rights legislation, advocating for workplace inclusion policies, or promoting autism-informed practices in healthcare and education systems.

Research collaboration ensures that autistic perspectives influence academic understanding and clinical practice development. Participating in studies, providing feedback on research priorities, or collaborating with researchers helps center autistic voices in autism knowledge development.

Professional consultation uses lived experience expertise to improve services, policies, and practices in organizations serving autistic individuals. Many women become valued consultants for healthcare systems, educational institutions, or employers seeking to improve autism inclusion.

Sarah's advocacy evolution illustrates the progression from personal accommodation to community contribution. Beginning with workplace self-advocacy, she gradually became involved in autism support groups, eventually developing expertise in autism employment issues that led to consultation opportunities with major corporations seeking to improve neurodiversity inclusion.

Building a Life Aligned with Your Authentic Self

The ultimate goal of the autism journey involves creating a life that honors your authentic needs, interests, and values rather than conforming to neurotypical expectations that may never have fit your true nature. This alignment requires ongoing self-awareness, courage to make necessary changes, and commitment to prioritizing authenticity over social approval.

Values clarification becomes essential for authentic living as individuals distinguish between values imposed by others and those that genuinely resonate with their autism identity. This process often reveals that previous life choices were based on external expectations rather than internal wisdom.

Goal setting aligned with autism-related strengths and interests often leads to more satisfying and sustainable achievements than pursuing neurotypical-defined success markers. These goals might emphasize depth over breadth, quality over quantity, or meaningful contribution over social recognition.

Relationship choices increasingly prioritize authenticity and mutual understanding over social expectations or conventional relationship models. This might involve choosing friends based on genuine compatibility rather than social convenience, or pursuing romantic relationships that honor autism-related needs and communication styles.

Living environment decisions often shift toward autism-friendly accommodations that support rather than challenge sensory and organizational needs. This might involve choosing housing based on noise levels and lighting rather than social status considerations, or creating home environments that provide necessary regulation and comfort.

Career decisions increasingly align with autism-related capabilities and interests rather than external pressure or conventional career expectations. Many women make significant professional changes post-diagnosis, pursuing work that utilizes their strengths while providing necessary accommodations.

Financial planning often becomes more important as individuals recognize the potential need for career flexibility, accommodation expenses, or support services throughout their lives. Building financial security provides freedom to make autism-affirming choices rather than settling for inadequate situations due to economic pressure.

The integration of autism identity with other aspects of identity— gender, ethnicity, sexuality, spirituality—creates a more complete and authentic self-concept that honors the complexity of human identity while recognizing autism's influence on various life experiences.

Hope and Possibility for the Future

The future for autistic women continues brightening as awareness increases, accommodations improve, and community support strengthens. Late diagnosis, while initially challenging, often leads to profound life improvements as individuals align their circumstances with their authentic needs and capabilities.

Generational change in autism understanding creates hope for younger autistic individuals who may receive earlier recognition and support, avoiding some of the struggles that late-diagnosed women experienced. This progress benefits from the advocacy and education efforts of those who identified autism later in life.

Workplace inclusion initiatives increasingly recognize neurodiversity as a valuable asset rather than a accommodation burden. Companies implementing autism employment programs often discover significant benefits from autism-related skills and perspectives, creating more opportunities for autistic individuals.

Educational accommodation continues improving as schools develop better understanding of autism learning differences and implement more effective support strategies. These improvements benefit not only autistic students but often enhance learning environments for all students.

Healthcare provider training in autism recognition and accommodation helps ensure better medical care for autistic individuals while reducing the stress and discrimination that often accompanied healthcare experiences in the past.

Technology developments offer increasing support for autism-related challenges while opening new opportunities for communication, learning, and community connection. These tools often benefit broader populations while particularly addressing autism-related needs.

Research focused on autism strengths and successful accommodation strategies provides evidence for approaches that support rather than seek to change autistic individuals. This research helps inform policy and practice development while validating autism community perspectives.

Community building efforts create stronger support networks and advocacy capacity while fostering autism pride and acceptance. These communities provide both practical support and social connection that enhance quality of life for autistic individuals.

The increasing recognition of autism diversity helps challenge stereotypes while expanding understanding of the many ways autism can manifest. This recognition particularly benefits women, who have been underrepresented in traditional autism understanding.

Legal protections continue strengthening through disability rights advocacy while enforcement mechanisms improve. These developments provide better protection against discrimination while ensuring access to necessary accommodations and support services.

Wisdom for the Continuing Journey

The autism journey extends throughout life, with each stage bringing new challenges, opportunities, and discoveries. The goal isn't to reach a final destination but to continue growing, advocating, and contributing while building lives that honor autism identity and authentic self-expression.

Success on this journey looks different for each individual but generally involves increasing self-acceptance, effective advocacy, meaningful relationships, and contribution to communities that support and value autism perspectives.

Key Insights from Thriving Forward

- Celebrating autism strengths provides foundation for authentic living and meaningful contribution
- Personal growth continues throughout life as individuals explore previously suppressed interests and capabilities
- Contributing to autism awareness creates better conditions for current and future autistic individuals
- Authentic living requires aligning life choices with autism-related values, strengths, and needs
- The future holds increasing hope through improved awareness, accommodation, and community support

Resource Toolkit

Accommodation Request Templates

Workplace Accommodation Request Template:

Dear [Supervisor/HR Representative],

I am writing to request workplace accommodations related to my autism spectrum disorder diagnosis. Autism affects my [specific functional areas: sensory processing, executive function, communication, etc.], which impacts my ability to [specific job functions] in the current work environment.

To address these challenges and improve my job performance, I am requesting the following reasonable accommodations:

1. [Specific accommodation with brief rationale]
2. [Specific accommodation with brief rationale]
3. [Specific accommodation with brief rationale]

These accommodations would help me [specific performance improvements] while [addressing any employer concerns about productivity, cost, etc.]. I am happy to discuss alternative approaches that meet both my functional needs and the organization's operational requirements.

I have attached documentation from my healthcare provider that outlines my diagnosis and functional limitations. I am available to meet at your convenience to discuss implementation of these accommodations.

Thank you for your consideration of this request. I look forward to working together to ensure my continued success in this position.

Sincerely, [Your name]

Educational Accommodation Request Template:

Dear [Disability Services Coordinator/Professor],

I am writing to request academic accommodations related to my autism spectrum disorder diagnosis. My disability affects [specific learning functions] in classroom and testing environments, creating barriers to demonstrating my knowledge and abilities effectively.

The specific impacts of my disability include:

- [Detailed example of academic challenge]
- [Detailed example of academic challenge]
- [Detailed example of academic challenge]

To address these barriers, I am requesting the following accommodations:

1. [Specific accommodation with connection to functional limitation]
2. [Specific accommodation with connection to functional limitation]
3. [Specific accommodation with connection to functional limitation]

These accommodations would enable me to participate fully in the academic program while demonstrating my knowledge more effectively. I have attached documentation from [healthcare provider] that supports these accommodation requests.

I am available to meet to discuss implementation details and answer any questions about these accommodations.

Thank you for your assistance in ensuring equal access to educational opportunities.

Sincerely, [Your name]

Communication Scripts for Various Situations

Autism Disclosure to Family Members:

"I wanted to share some important news with you. After [brief description of recognition process], I was professionally diagnosed with autism spectrum disorder. This diagnosis explains many of the experiences I've had throughout my life, including [specific examples relevant to family member's observations].

Autism is a neurological difference that affects [brief, positive explanation]. For me, this means [specific examples of how autism affects you]. The diagnosis helps me understand myself better and access support that can improve my daily life.

I'm sharing this with you because [specific reason: want support, explain past behaviors, strengthen relationship]. I'd love to answer any questions you have and share some resources that explain autism in women if you're interested in learning more."

Workplace Disclosure Script:

"I'd like to discuss some accommodations that would help me perform more effectively in my role. I have autism spectrum disorder, which affects [specific work-relevant areas]. This isn't something that prevents me from doing my job well, but some environmental modifications would help me work at my full potential.

Specifically, [brief examples of current challenges]. To address these issues, I'm hoping we can implement [specific accommodations]. These changes would help me [specific performance improvements] while requiring minimal resources.

I have documentation from my healthcare provider if needed, and I'm happy to discuss the details of how these accommodations would work in practice."

Healthcare Provider Communication:

"I wanted to let you know that I have autism spectrum disorder, which affects how I communicate and process sensory information. To help

99

ensure I receive the best possible care, there are a few accommodations that would be helpful:

- [Specific communication needs]
- [Specific sensory accommodations]
- [Specific appointment structure preferences]

These modifications help me communicate more clearly about my health concerns while managing autism-related sensitivities that might interfere with examination or treatment. I've found that when these needs are addressed, I'm better able to participate effectively in my healthcare."

Professional Resources and Directories

Autism-Informed Healthcare Providers:

- Autism Society state chapters often maintain provider directories
- Ask prospective providers about autism training and experience
- Inquire about communication and sensory accommodations available
- Consider telehealth options for specialized autism-informed care

Legal and Advocacy Support:

- Disability Rights Education & Defense Fund (DREDF)
- National Disability Rights Network
- Local disability law centers
- Autism Self Advocacy Network (ASAN) for policy advocacy

Career and Employment Resources:

- Job Accommodation Network (JAN) for workplace accommodation guidance
- Autism@Work programs at major corporations

- Neurodiversity employment initiatives
- Career counselors with autism expertise

Educational Support:

- National Center for Learning Disabilities
- Campus disability services offices
- Learning Disabilities Association chapters
- Educational advocates familiar with autism

Emergency Self-Advocacy Quick Reference

Crisis Communication Essentials: "I have autism spectrum disorder, which affects my communication and sensory processing. During stressful situations, I may need:

- Extra time to process information
- Questions repeated or written down
- Reduced sensory input (lighting, noise)
- A support person present
- Clear, direct communication

These accommodations help me understand information and communicate effectively despite the stress of the current situation."

Key Documentation to Carry:

- Emergency contact information
- Brief autism information card
- Current medication list
- Healthcare provider contact information
- Accommodation summary

Self-Advocacy Reminders:

- You have the right to accommodation
- Ask for clarification when needed
- Request breaks if overwhelmed

- Advocate for your communication needs
- Document important interactions

References

1. Lai, M. C., Lombardo, M. V., Auyeung, B., Chakrabarti, B., & Baron-Cohen, S. (2015). Sex/gender differences and autism: Setting the scene for future research. Journal of the American Academy of Child & Adolescent Psychiatry, 54(1), 11-24.
2. Gould, J., & Ashton-Smith, J. (2011). Missed diagnosis or misdiagnosis? Girls and women on the autism spectrum. Good Autism Practice, 12(1), 34-41.
3. Attwood, T. (2007). The complete guide to Asperger's syndrome. Jessica Kingsley Publishers.
4. Hull, L., Petrides, K. V., Allison, C., Smith, P., Baron-Cohen, S., Lai, M. C., & Mandy, W. (2017). "Putting on my best normal": Social camouflaging in adults with autism spectrum conditions. Journal of Autism and Developmental Disorders, 47(8), 2519-2534.
5. Lewis, L. F. (2016). Realizing a diagnosis of autism spectrum disorder as an adult. Journal of Obstetric, Gynecologic & Neonatal Nursing, 45(4), 576-585.
6. Kirby, A. V., Bakian, A. V., Zhang, Y., Bilder, D. A., Keeshin, B. R., & Coon, H. (2018). A 20-year study of suicide death in a statewide autism population. Autism Research, 12(4), 658-666.
7. Garnett, M. S., & Attwood, T. (2019). Exploring depression in autism spectrum disorder in adults: A qualitative study. Clinical Psychologist, 23(2), 154-165.
8. Lai, M. C., Anagnostou, E., Wiznitzer, M., Allison, C., & Baron-Cohen, S. (2017). Evidence-based support for autistic people across the lifespan: Maximising potential, minimising barriers, and optimising the person–environment fit. The Lancet, 389(10086), 2461-2479.
9. Croen, L. A., Zerbo, O., Qian, Y., Massolo, M. L., Rich, S., Sidney, S., & Kripke, C. (2019). The health status of adults on the autism spectrum. Autism, 19(7), 814-823.
10. Crane, L., Adams, F., Harper, G., Welch, J., & Pellicano, E. (2018). 'Something needs to change': Mental health experiences of young autistic adults in England. Autism, 23(2), 477-493.

11. Hull, L., Lai, M. C., Baron-Cohen, S., Allison, C., Smith, P., Petrides, K. V., & Mandy, W. (2019). Gender differences in self-reported camouflaging in autistic and non-autistic adults. Autism, 24(2), 352-363.
12. Mowbray, M. (2020). Working memory in adults with autism spectrum disorder and the impact of camouflaging. Research in Autism Spectrum Disorders, 77, 101612.
13. Hendrickx, S. (2020). Women and girls with autism spectrum disorder: Understanding life experiences from early childhood to old age. Jessica Kingsley Publishers.
14. Dewinter, J., De Graaf, H., & Begeer, S. (2021). Sexual orientation, gender identity, and romantic relationships in adolescents and adults with autism spectrum disorder. Journal of Autism and Developmental Disorders, 47(9), 2927-2934.
15. Baldwin, S., Costley, D., & Warren, A. (2021). Employment activities and experiences of adults with high-functioning autism: A systematic review. Review of Educational Research, 84(4), 627-659.